Collected Poems

THE GERMAN LIST

THOMAS BERNHARD
Collected Poems

TRANSLATED BY JAMES REIDEL

LONDON NEW YORK CALCUTTA

This publication was supported by a grant from
the Goethe-Institut India

Grateful acknowledgement is given to *Artful Dodge* for 'An
Evening', 'Living and Dead', 'My Parents' House' and 'The
year is like a year a thousand years ago'; *Conjunctions* for *Ave
Virgil*, 'Beyond the Trees Is another World', 'I Know that in
the Bushes Are Souls', 'In silva salus', 'In the Grass', *The Insane
The Inmates*, 'No Tree', 'One Day I Will Walk into the Forest',
'Rot', 'The Wind'; *Greensboro Review* for 'Torment' (under the
title 'Agony'); and Princeton University Press for *In Hora
Mortis* and *Under the Iron of the Moon*.

Seagull Books, 2017

The poems in this volume were originally published in Thomas
Bernhard, *Gesammelte Gedichte* © Suhrkamp Verlag, Frankfurt am
main, 1991; and *Gedichte* © Suhrkamp Verlag, Berlin, 2015.

First published in English translation by Seagull Books, 2017

ISBN   978 0 8574 2 426 6

British Library Cataloguing-in-Publication Data
A catalogue record for this book is available
from the British Library.

Typeset by Seagull Books, Calcutta, India
Printed and bound by Maple Press, York, Pennsylvania, USA

Contents

Early Poems
(1952–1956)

My World Play

It's the same look a thousand times
through the window at my world play.
An apple tree in the pale green,
and above thousands of blossoms,
resting against the sky like this,
a band of clouds, which stretches far . . .
the afternoon cries of children,
as if the world were just childhood;
a wagon creaks, an old man stands
and waits for his day to pass by.
From the chimney atop the roof
our smoke faintly drifts to the clouds . . .
The chickens feed, the roosters crow—
yes, nothing but strange people walk
in the sunshine, year in, year out,
walking on by our old homeplace.
The laundry flutters on the line
over which you dream being happy,
in the cellar a poor man weeps,
for he can no longer sing a song . . .
It's more or less like this by day,
and with each new toll of the bell
there is the same look a thousand times
through the window at my world play.

(1952)

Summer

I lie in the world on my back,
I need no house, I need no tent,
I am so free and unworried.
My life is worthy of this hour.

With morning a band of clouds drifts
Downwards to the edge of the sky,
The wave rushes, this is the year,
Which was never so delightful.

And the smell of the earth returns
Borne along by the springtime breeze,
The hour rests, the country is far
And is bringing back this blissfulness.

I am so far and I am so near,
I don't know what happened to me,
I dream away and I live on
And hover with the angels there.

(1952)

The Farmer

How he makes
His steps,
Always measured
And deliberate,
Down field,
Up field,
Always near the
Sun's path . . .
Seed grain,
Wheat shimmer,
Fallow fields,
Dancing snowflakes,
He always lives
Near to God,
And daily makes
Our bread . . .
He always says
His prayers,
When he stands
Upon the earth,
Firm and waking,
Hard and broad,
Over every
Play of time . . .

(1952)

The Wanderer

Here I walk and will every day never come back,
For I bear in my hands the world and its joy.

And a thousand flowers are around me here,
And I take the hill, in this way still more come,

And they come like lights, and they shine so placid—
The reaches of the sky complement this image.

The crowns of the trees are one with the wind
And they rustle overhead and once more swiftly

A wave slips away into this blissful year,
Which was the beginning and the end of hope . . .

Thus will I just wander, for I am ready,
For I let it play, this time of happiness,

And I listen to the earth and shun the house—
Thus do I run out of these worlds in the end . . .

(1952)

Fisherman on the Chiemsee

Where the waves batter against the shoreline,
Wild ducks are swimming into their lines,
The fisherman has to carry his nets,
He goes forth singing down to the boats.

In rowing his he takes every broad stretch,
The clear sky is mirrored on the lake,
In the centre of these wonderful times
He glances up at the placid heights . . .

Within his nets he has a thousand lives,
The fine day sinks into the mountains,
A thousand dreams are surrounding him,
Which he may not entirely catch.

It is evening, silently he rows back,
Every light is slowly extinguished,
Finally he walks back bringing his fish,
Over strange fields, into his small house . . .

(1952)

All Souls

To Agatha Wibe

With the wind, the little girls are singing,
This unknown choir under the steeple,
The women emerge in their dark dresses
Always quiet, coming from the night.

In their eyes resides the poor's suffering,
The born-with agony of this earth,
In their steps and in their making the sign,
It lies hundredfold, a thousand times.

With their candles every soul is lit up—
In their wreaths they tied their happiness,
They stand before the gravesites and they know:
Before long our friends are coming back,

Coming inside again in these long hours
At the door and finding a place to sit,
Coming rich and becoming with the years
Always further more into our midst . . .

(1952)

The Conversation

The Young Man:
So, as though with golden wings,
Metamorphosed and gone,
I float with a thousand things,
Where gods are singing to me
And I have time and sense . . .

The Old Man:
These may be beautiful times—
You will need a good tent . . .
You can never go striding
Off into eternity,
For you will get homesick . . .

The Young Man:
I can sip from a thousand cups
The light of a mild sun . . .
O world of a thousand pains,
Allow me to pay my debt,
Then am I yours and whole . . .

The Old Man:
All living things are varied—
As I am an old man,
Who has made friends with this peace,
Which is shunned by all the world,
The one I can still love . . .

(1952)

O Deep Night . . .

O deep night, O night in the snow,
Through which I walk calmly thinking . . .
In a luminous boat the moon
Rows high overhead on its path,
And it drips amid the fir trees
The golden waves of a broad sea . . .
And all is still . . . through shrub and tree
The gentle dream of this earth flows . . .
O deep night, O night in the snow,
Through which I walk calmly thinking . . .

(1952)

Gulls

In the tidal waves of the storms
The dark city sinks to us,
The towers loom up eerily
By night, which has no more light . . .

The water rushes down aslant,
Petrified the branches crack,
The images go fuming down
And sometimes they will hold fast.

Stark on the beams of the bridges
The gulls perch scattered about,
They are tearing flesh in pieces
And then sail lovely and far.

At last their multitudes alone
Inhabit the dark shoreline,
Strangely they swoop down in a clear,
Terrible sigh on land . . .

(1953)

January

Into the snow sinks
This beautiful land . . .
As though of glass it shatters
From enormous ancient firs.
The clouds wander,
The snowflakes fall
From enormous
Heavenly milk cans . . .
The sacred kings
File past
With gold and incense and myrrh . . .
They can, so it is said,
Not stray . . .
Their journey goes far
Uphill over snow—
Which crunches of dreams and time,
Of winter and waking,
Crystal hard—
Which crunches of weeping and laughter . . .
Three kings wander, and you
And yours . . .
The suns wander and shine.

(1954)

To Have Only a Landscape . . .

To have only a landscape, I think, and a house,
A river and this view of the mountains,
And over the winds, far over the valley
An empire, much greater than our earth.
I would not sicken, I would survive.
I could see the deepest depths.
I would bear pain and the highest bliss.
I would find my way out again.
Thus I thought yesterday: a river, a house
Where life flows and gives out.
A field deep in a land of fog,
A plough guided by one's own hand—
Just a landscape, just a house,
Where the graves stand to the wind,
A land, much deeper than our earth.
And I lived in the darkness downstream.

(1954)

Stream of Being

For a fleeting moment we all stand in place,
Watching while life is gushing away,
Standing today alone at the threshold,
Drifting tomorrow upon the blank wave
Downstream by now, and it flows and flows.

No one can stop it, no one will stop it,
Dams will burst and it goes flowing onwards.
Trusted images, catchwords and forms,
Entire worlds go down with that which is old
Leaving not a trace at the beginning.

Hardly opened today, hardly enjoyed,
It sinks back into oblivion.
It is transparent and accessible,
It is a stream long since flowing downwards—
And you call it happiness.

(1954)

Salzburg

Your bright towers in the clear early morning,
You warm wind, you tree in its senescence,
The cathedral dome reaches into space
And casts its shadow calmly, with no effort

Above the streets and the columns' capitals.—
In tranquil courtyards the new grape vines grow rank.
The sunshine tries a thousand times over
In the quiet tinkling of a clear fountain.

Thus does light ripple across the flat rooftops,
And flashes like fire and soon turns to stone.
The entire city drinks from the sun's beaker

And revels far into the distant green leaves
And withers into the sky all alone
And becomes music in the pigeons' reeling.

(1954)

In the Cathedral

Heaven's tapestry is unfurled before you.
It means there are just more wide steps to climb now
And before the portals a time for silence
Until someone walks inside the dome with you.

O bright sunny day, one which swelters outside—
Where did you find the mercy over the years,
To walk so cheerful and unceasing and straight,
Before God, the one who looked after you once?

The walls do not reproach you as tyrants would.
Here a peace is rising above the altars,
As though no fighting, no war had taken place,

Which fools had thought up once stupid with passion.
By golden crucifixes, in the sweet coils
Of precious incense, is where you will find rest . . .

(1954)

In the Courtyard of St Peter's

A peel of bells comes out of the blue
And goes trembling off along the hot walls,
And at a wall must end to itself,
For the smooth stone is completely deaf.

Life floods softly in nevertheless,
And comes guardedly out of the high rooms
Of the palace and beams of light shimmer
As though into a crimson-filled shrine.

The black monks walk with their heads bowed low
Around the fountain, while up in the trees
The baby swallows are nesting in dreams.

And they are praying without looking up,
As someone stops before a blue noon sky
Miraculously and is silent.

(1954)

Cemetery in Seekirchen (I)

It is written: merchant, farmer, husband.
Here one individual had been born once,
Here a hundred were lost in a single night—
The war captivated them in its spell.

Who sits on the gravestone and lacks courage?
There is a secret apparent in the stone,
There are those who will laugh, those who weep here
And human blood will be boiling over.

It is written: merchant, farmer, husband.
It is written, where it was and when they died—
It begins one day, the stone starts to speak,

But no one says how miserably doomed they were.
The war had them captivated in its spell . . .
The sheaves smell sweet coming off the threshing floor.

(1954)

Old Landscape

An aged landscape, everyone finds home.
Who flees no more from murder and fire and storms,
Returning to where he came from to recite
His rhymes at the high towers of the church?

O young city in the old Occident!
Once my father came only to look at you,
From the east here in the first light of morning
During your summer, on the bright shoreline.

Italy's gentleness in the German stone!
Music is performed in every palace,
And gods are waging war against the vulgar.

Just like my father did, others will as well
Stop here in distant nights for respite,
And wander unceasingly before your face.

(1954)

St Sebastian in Linzergasse

Noon bows low to the street's oppressiveness,
Here the earth has been trapped inside—
The fog sometimes wanders far and close,
And one of the church pews creak in the dark.

The young women stand up and take long steps,
Wreaths of woven flowers on pale brows.
Along with the stones, starve heart and mind,
For solemnities a thousand years old.

The air heavy from the cracking of bones,
A bell's sound rises into the chapel—
From somewhere off I hear mothers . . .

Paracelsus, the noblemen, ladies—
All stare bewildered from their long dreams
Into the green of ancient almond trees.

(1954)

Cloister Walk in Nonnberg Abbey (I)

The world in the evening, for this I enter.
The young nuns come to this place and they watch here,
And early dreams lie entirely in the grey.
These young women must feel very happy.

The fountain splashes its song wonderfully
By day and night; the fresh dew falls downwards
As though in the tired lilacs of a May night.
But you look upwards as the clouds tear past

And a blackbird twitters inside the arches.
You see the sun itself in solitude
Setting around columns a thousand years old.

You are a stranger here upon every path.
It is not far to roses and to God—
And the deep night brings with it a boon of stars.

(1954)

Danube Harbour

Where the ships lie spread out at anchor
The smoke rises in the midday blue,
Men are shouting, the white pennants flutter,
Glass and cable twinkle from the sun.
Outside the warehouses the sirens blow,
The dogs are barking and the crane groans.
The luminous bands of clouds tear and stretch
Endlessly before the railroad tracks.
From the bridge one can look out much farther,
All the way to a sea of grey mist—
From a long distance away the trim sterns
Of new ships are sailing towards the east.

(1954)

Song of the Farmgirl

I saw so many faces—
They give no rest;
God's lights give light
To all the good people.

It's as if I died today
The very first death.
There goes my dream through the vast
Far-too-early red dawn . . .

Grant that it will be evening,
Bring on the good, long night—
For the hard earth made me weak
Made me weak and made me tired.

(1954)

Homecoming

The way out is through the plain,
they are all strange, the tree and the house.
My land rises and falls, on dark hills
I see clouds in motion like Graces . . .
The valleys flow into the green,
where the aging country folk toil.
Slowly their farms become smaller.
Soon it will be good and evening,
soon I will be there, just that band
of hills and that faraway ridge,
the onion-domed towers, that dot
soaring in the blue—what a day!
O what a wonderful moment!
Not one thought is looking backwards . . .
The world behind me was not good.
It still runs in my blood endlessly,
and once more I feel how it hurts
as my soul stumbles on homewards . . .
Go! Go! The darkness falls like scales.
Thus does man climb out of his grave.
The hay, the calm—I'm allowed in—
So should it be for all one's life!

(1955)

Rectory Garden in Henndorf

The sunlight leans against the trees,
and the window takes a rest.
The fragrance of our apples spreads
once more into the wide world.

Leaves are playing along the wall.
Somewhere a child still weeps ...
Through the secluded garden
the evening wind goes dreamlike.

In the threshold of the stairs,
my sister peels potatoes
and she dreams of the white blossoms
on the ancient cherry tree.

A bell is tolling from somewhere,
and there is the smell of bread,
and one hears the maidservants pray—
Around the table is no want.

(1955)

With Evening

Rain has enshrouded the trees,
and my child is up,
waiting for the sun to shine.
Outside the stream roars.

Across the pasture the day
goes like an old man.
Over there in the dark grove
the millwheel still turns.

There is no one with your face.
Child, don't bother me—
Outside burns a wandering light
And the gate slams shut.

With evening, before the night,
when the cold winds blow,
where the firwood cracks, you see
not one person pass.

(1955)

To Wake Up and to Have a House . . .

To wake up and to have a house—
This anywhere and any way!
To keep digging for a crop,
to possess a well of your own—
You'll never get it!

To be here creating a beginning,
to get to sleep in the night—
to have all your streams running
unceasingly, inwardly deep
and not thought to death.

You longed to discover peace and quiet,
to have a place in this world—
to establish your own landscape,
to tie up the sheaves of your fate
underneath your sky . . .

No more sinking demandingly in plaints—
to live through the day and night,
to carry spring inside one's soul,
to build bridges that are near you
for the final load.

(1955)

Cloister (II)

The world in the evening, for this I enter.
The young nuns come to this place and here they watch
The early dreams, those faraway turning blue.
These young women must feel very happy.

The fountain splashes its song wonderfully
by day and night; the fresh dew falls downwards
as though in the tired lilacs of a May night.
But you look upwards as the clouds tear past

And a blackbird twitters inside the arches.
You see the sun itself in solitude
Setting around columns a thousand years old.

You are a stranger here upon every path.
It is not far to roses and to God—
And the deep night brings with it a boon of stars.

(1955)

The Villagers

I say to the baker: How long do I eat your bread?
I say to the cobbler: How long do I walk in your shoes?
I say to the tailor: Your coat will no longer fit me!
I say to the priest: How long do I pray for me not to feel
shame?
I say to them all: How very afraid I am outside their houses,
and love is weak, it is so weak,
such that the coat of the tailor will no more fit,
no more,
and the shoes will pinch me, and the pork
of the butcher I will eat with disgust.
I see through everything and ask: Who made you?
You miraculous creatures, who has taught you the lie,
your presence?
You children, you old men, you who kill with the wind
everywhere?
You who are like the father of my father?
You who are like the mother of my mother?
Endlessly!
Endlessly!
Who made you?
I can no longer see the face, the one on your necks
growing

like the sunflower which sucked the sap from all the
others during
the past year and was like the sun—
You do not shine!

(1955)

[Two poems stricken from *On Earth and In Hell*—Trans.]

You Unknown Fathers of My Fame

Brewers, butchers, wheat brothers of the world,
whose earth you peopled between the green of the hills
and the blackness of the Plaike mountain sky,
be at peace and give me a sign!
Brewers, butchers, wheat brothers of the world,
I hear your voices and your song,
with which I can destroy cities for your immortality,
which rises from the streams
in October
and when the snow falls!
Brewers, butchers, wheat brothers of the world,
you unknown fathers of my fame,
slaughterers of wretchedness,
give the wind a sign,
with which I can rid myself of my sadness before I go mad!

Song for Young Males

(*To sing accompanied by guitar, for that anger when one has no money and no woman*)

Tonight, tomorrow morning
We want bread and a black smoked ham,
And drink red wine along with that,
Tonight, tomorrow morning

Tonight, tomorrow morning
We want to give our butchers praise
And the sows in their black pigpens,
Tonight, tomorrow morning

Tonight, tomorrow morning
We want our brains to be stopped up
And our skulls to feel beaten on,
Tonight, tomorrow morning

Tonight, tomorrow morning
We want that hole there in the moon
Our cousin found two years ago,
Tonight, tomorrow morning

Tonight, tomorrow morning
We want to cheat on our own flesh
And go ploughing the red furrows . . .
Tonight, tomorrow morning

Tonight, tomorrow morning
We want to forget our women
And the ones we will never have . . .
Tonight, tomorrow morning

Tonight, tomorrow morning
We want some black frocks for ourselves
And go hide behind Jesus Christ
Tonight, tomorrow morning.

On Earth and in Hell

Of the one you never heard a thing.
And what we've heard of the other is
the word
of death.

Charles Péguy

The Day of Faces

Tomorrow is the day of faces. They will
    rise like dust
    and burst into laughter.
Tomorrow is the day of faces which have
    fallen into the potato soil. I can-
    not deny that I
    am to blame for this dying of the sprouts.
I am to blame!
Tomorrow is the day of faces which bear my torment
    on their foreheads,
    who are vested in my day's work.
Tomorrow is the day of faces which as flesh
    dance on the churchyard wall
    and point out Hell for me.
    Why must I see Hell? Is there no other way
to God?

A voice: There is no other way! And this way
    leads to the day of faces,
    it leads through Hell.

Beyond the Trees
Is Another World

My Great-Grandfather Was a Lard Merchant

My great-grandfather was a lard merchant,
and today
some still recall him
between Henndorf and Thalgau,
Seekirchen and Köstendorf,
and they hear his voice
and draw
together at his table,
which was also the table of gentlemen.
1881, in the spring,
he made up his mind for life: he planted
grape vines along a wall outside the house
and called the beggars together;
his wife, Maria, the one with the black ribbon,
gave him a further thousand years.
He invented the music of pigs
and the fire of bitterness,
he spoke of the wind
and of the wedding of the dead.
He would give me not one slice of speck
for my despair.

On the Black Coffins of Farmland

On the black coffins of farmland
    it is written that I must die in the winter,
abandoned by my suns and by the whispering of pails,
    those full of milk,
torture and finality speaking amid the blows of the March
                                      winds,
    which annihilated me with the thought
of apple blossoms and the magic of threshing floors!
    Never have I destroyed a night with curse words
and tears, but this time, this insane time,
    is going to extinguish me
with its dry, knife-sharp poetry!
    I will not have to suffer the solitude alone but, rather,
drive the cattle of my fathers and mothers through thousands
                                     of years!
    I will have to create rain
and snow and mother's love
    for my crime, and glorify the anger
which ruins the grain in one's own fields!
    I will summon together the merchants and Saturday
                              whores to a woodlot,
and bequeath this land, this sorry land,
    with its wild despair!

I will let a thousand suns enter my
     hunger! Tomorrow I will
create ephemera for immortality,
     near the fountains and towers and far from
the craftsmen,
     on a morning which is sick of my suffering
and when nothing happens but the passing away of stars . . .
     . . . there I will speak with those who despair
and leave everything behind,
     what contempt, bitterness and sorrow was in this world.

November Sacrifice

I am unworthy of these fields and furrows,
    unworthy of this sky that scores its wild signs
for another thousand years into my mind,
    unworthy of these forests, whose shower will burst
as I age with the thunderstorms of cities.
    I am unworthy of that mother on the hillside and
                        unworthy
of the farmers who plough through their day
    with cows and pear trees, liquor and scythes.
I am unworthy of these mountains and steeples,
    unworthy of a single starry night
and unworthy of every beggars' footpath
    which ends in sadness.
I am unworthy of this grass that cools my limbs,
    the tree trunks in their cruel deformities,
which the north drives with rain
    and the shadows of the boys
who offer their November sacrifice to the cider
    amid the black mounds that bear my ephemeralness.
I am unworthy of these processions
    which May brings forth between apple blossoms,
of milk and of honey, of fame and of rot
    which are promised to me.
I am unworthy among the priests, the butchers and
                        merchants,

unworthy for the prophecies of these gardens,
unworthy of the Sunday which spews its sweet smoke into
the blue.
I am unworthy of those abandoned red-pimpled girls
in this thousand-year-old landscape,
whose bread tastes of hunger and dead people,
futility and the grief of mothers
who cannot escape their torment,
the torment of the forgotten whom the sun burns in the
fields.
I am unworthy of the blackbird, unworthy of the
creaking of the millwheel.
Unworthy, I carry on my act at the banks of the river,
which wants to know nothing of the villages.
I am unworthy of these souls who in clouds and bushes
talk to one another about the land in flower,
about the dying of heaven's music,
of the enormous desolations sweeping over the hills,
the stormy winters of the world scudding impatiently ahead.

Rot

.

Imperishable as the sun I saw the earth
    when I fell back to sleep which seeks my father,
who brought the last wind's message
    into my wretchedness, which grieves for his fame,
the fame of which he said: 'Great talents
    come to nought tomorrow . . .'
Immortal stand the forests which once filled the night
    with their lament and their talk
of cider and doom. Only the wind
    was above the wheat ears, while spring lived on
amid this sweet rot.
    The snow turned against me and made
my limbs shiver at the sight
    of the restless north, which resembles an enormous,
                                   inexhaustible
cemetery, the cemetery for the prisoners
    of this triumph, which crept
into every wayside cross, into every field stone
    and into every country road and church, whose spires
                                          rose
against God and against the wedding party,
    which gathered around their cask of wine to
drink it up with pig's laughter.
    How I watched these dead in the village, on benches

eating red meat with swollen bellies,
    slurring the hymns of March beer,
the rot slinking through the tavern garden
    amid the dull braying of the trombone . . .
I heard the deep breath of depravity
            between the hills . . .
    Imperishable as the sun I saw the earth
whose August was sick and irretrievable
    for me and my brothers who learnt their craft
better than I, such that I am harassed
    by those millions of the beggar class and no longer
do I find a tree for my insane conversations.
    I went from a night of hell
to a night of heaven,
    not knowing who must crush my life
before it is too late, to speak of fame and courage,
    of poverty and that earthly despair
of the flesh that will annihilate me . . .

In the Villages of the Flachgau

Only shadows are there where you saw the first merchants,
the filth between their teeth, the shoes
which were too big and inexplicable to your eyes,
only shadows are there where churches opened and old
                                        grey men
buried their fame for a better life
when they lived only for their members and for smoke and
                                        wine
in the flesh of the sweet country taprooms.

Only shadows are there where they watered down the honey
and sold off sick cows on nameless grey towns, where they
robbed the mothers of grass and life and
taught their children to die on forsaken hills.
There are only shadows and inhospitable benches, which
                                        for my flesh,
so much are you plagued too, denies the fame
which it is entitled to after its journeys.

Only shadows are there where they don't praise the
                                        butterflies
and don't the poetry of the pigs and don't the day
of cups and of twilight, which from the forests
joined in their melancholy, where they don't glorify

seas, cities, warriors of other lands and don't weep
upon an unquenched day in barricaded temples, where the
                                                      sun
fleetingly reaches the dusty rubble of the world.

Only shadows are there where they pursued dreams
                              without tiring of blood
and grief, where they went to fairs sick from meat and from
                                              gambling,
into churches and to the dance, to the parish priests often
                                        in disgust, but
to their point of origin surely in fame, and where they
                                              listened
in bed at night to the impermanence, which they
handed down to us in this world no longer theirs.

Down Falls the Rain on the Black Forests

Down falls the rain on the black forests,
thus do the doors shut on my hours
As though I would not have risen from the night,
from the depths of this grey day's work,
angry with the last friends of my
weak, despicable soul,
Which already bears my father's sick fate.

Down falls the rain on the black forests,
hear the cry, one meant for your sun, that tired cry
letting itself be driven through the wet tree trunks
strangely lamenting a bitter evening wind.
From hungry and dim eyes at night
The wonders of these early days rise
and limbs stretch beneath the rooftops
into the clutches of your listless poetry.

Down falls the rain on the black forests
and I search for the dream which I praised
only yesterday, which pressed down my wet eyes
on this bed in this cold room,
where the gears of the clock destroyed my world
along with the last sweet whisper of peace,
which was for my beloved farmland.

What Will I Do . . .

What will I do
    when no barn begs for my presence any more,
when the hay is burnt in damp villages
    without crowning my life?
What will I do
    when the woods only grow in my imagination,
when the streams are only more empty, washed-out veins?

What will I do
    when no message comes from the grass any more?
What will I do
    when I am forgotten by everybody, by everybody . . . ?

Bring Me Schnapps, Fame and Love

Bring me schnapps, for I want to forget!
    Today I want to dissipate
every creature in me and every torment,—
    and with that eat fish and a slice of pork!

Bring me fame, then can I quietly kill myself
    before my soul swells up
and my lofty brain inflates
    and everyone takes me for a fool!

Bring me your love to the table,
    I want to drink it floating low in the sky,
a hundred pitchers, a thousand pitchers, every pitcher in the
                                                    world,—
    I want to be drowned in your love.

Captive

The raven caws.
 He has me captive.
Through the land I must
 always wander inside his cry.
The raven caws.
 He has me captive.
Yesterday he perched in the field and froze
 and my heart with him.
My heart will always be blacker,
 for it is covered up by black
wings.

The Morning Carries a Big Sack

The morning carries a big sack.
    I say to him: You are so old
that you need not feel contempt for me.
    Your shoes are torn.
Your coat had once belonged to me—

    I sit in a hole and await you,
not like the crone, not like the children, not
    like the pastor who after the sermon
descends to the wine and muddles the earth.
    I welcome you with the whip,
trembling, cruel and fragile,
    like a thistle in the sun's corona.

The Evening Is My Brother . . .

I

The evening is my brother, for I have seen
how the tree twisted around after me,
for I have heard
how the farmers shattered their cups
and wine spattered in their faces,
those who accused Jesus on the cross.

II

I will go forth and wash their feet
and pour their wine into new cups.
I will stand in the marketplace and wait
until they tear my suit of clothes from me
and pound my shoes into flesh,
with which I have led the way for a hundred years.

Crows

Soon autumn comes and rescues the birds,
in gloomy taprooms brother and sister harvest
corn schnapps for winter's supper.
In the black village the pig is chained.
In the fields the crows of pain perish.
We drink the beer of despair
and fold hands before the scorn of the father.
The earth tastes of strings of meat.
Smoke rises over the farms
and leaves the fear of the besotted farmers behind.
The pump handle caws before the rotted window . . .
But I am not afraid.

Beyond the Trees Is Another World

Beyond the trees is another world,
the river brings me the moans,
the river brings me the dreams,
the river keeps silent when I with evening in the forests
dream of the north . . .

Beyond the trees is another world,
which my father mistook for two birds,
which my mother bore home in a basket,
which my brother lost in sleep when he was seven years old
                                        and tired . . .

Beyond the trees is another world,
a grass which tasted of sorrow, a black sun,
a moon of the dead,
a nightingale that never ceased to lament
of bread and wine
and milk in big pitchers
during the night of the prisoners.

Beyond the trees is another world,
they walk down the long furrows
into the villages, into the forests of thousands of years,
tomorrow they ask for me,
for the music of my afflictions,

when the wheat rots, when nothing has remained
of yesterday, of their lodgings, sacristies and waiting rooms.

I want to leave them. I want to speak
with no one any more,
they have betrayed me, the field knows it, the sun
will vindicate me, I know, I have come too late . . .

Beyond the trees is another world,
there is another country fair,
the dead swim in the kettles of the farmers and around the
                                                    ponds
the speck gently melts from the red skeletons,
there the souls no longer dream of the millwheel,
and the wind understands
only the wind . . .

Beyond the trees is another world,
the land of rot, the land
of merchants,
a landscape of graves left behind for you
and you will annihilate, sleep horribly
and drink and sleep
from morning to evening, from evening to morning
and understand nothing any more, not the river and not the
                                                    sorrow;
for beyond the trees
        tomorrow,
and beyond the hills,
        tomorrow,
is another world.

The Burnt-Out Cities

The Cities beyond the Ponds

We have never seen the cities beyond the ponds
and never the fragile sorrow
of the loneliness of these sick people,
never felt the pain under the wings
of black birds passing overhead
after the performance of a painful October,
which sends its song from distant chimneys.

We have never seen the cities beyond the ponds
and never the lonely dying
of scores of people who in nineteen hundred and four
were still at home on the dance floor
and one day withered away in narrow rooms
and saw the night plunge from gloomy corridors
in this way, as this earth sadly would.

We have never seen the cities beyond the ponds
and never heard the lamenting of women
cleaning the dust of long years
from their books and their dresses.
Never has one of us seen this fame,
which dies in white noon squares amid the sounds
of a starving concert band.

Fragments from a Dying City

I

When I am tired, I bowl my brain across the square
and let the feet trample and set the vileness of the butchers to
psalms.
From the hole of a tram car I look into the sky,
distracted by the trembling of the leaves and the lip-twisting of
girls.
I flee into a milk bar where they sadly drink their breakfast
and think about the sun that no longer comes.
They sleep in their grey coats and foresee the death
of many a green hill.

II

I hear the calls of the birds under an open sky
and the brawling of a stream.
I straggle into our desolate village
and let the milk from a million udders rejoice!
I toss a thousand coins into the wedding chapel,
    which brings besotted farmers glory . . .

III

The lamps sound like red meat in the midnight streets,
and my language is the language of the wind,
which blows across the pasture as though upon the oldest day,

which brings the horrors of deserts and the desire of drunken
                                                    palm trees
to the fields of my father.

IV

I eat my bread at the window seat and
look into your face which looks like the meat of lions
and of annihilation.
I see your brain dripping down on the rotting tapestry of farm
                                                    villages,
which have never drunk up so much pain as in these days,

when I abandoned them and live off midnight's black honey
behind my liquefying eyes.

V

I did not call out to them, and yet they darken my voice.
But after all everyone knows that I forgot how to pray,
for I am rotting away on a day in August in the year 1952,
everyone knows that I am choking to death on my own flesh.

VI

No one hears my voice, which will annihilate me.
They will surround my house and come through my door and
                                                    call the names
to which I answer.
They will forget that I am the creator of grass too
and that I am the provider of milk and honey.—
And in a valley of sadness they will slay me
when snow and wind and spring come too late . . .

An Evening

An evening on which the scales are taken down,
    behind which tower mountains of meat and fruit,
    the continents of crumbling souls into dust,
an evening between the black trees of the park
    and the tired brayings of the municipal bandstands
    on the frozen asphalt of scourged summers, which echo
    not one breath of your eminence,
an evening of whirling birds and taciturn beggars
    on the side of the white parliament where once they
                  wanted to murder you
    because you shouted 'fatherland' and regarded their faces
                   with too little disdain,
an evening which is as cold as night before the village,
    between the trunks of trees up to their necks in snow,
an evening of closed milk bars whose smooth tabletops
    lead a desperate struggle against the tuning pegs of our
                   countrymen's guitars,
    closed churches, closed bordellos, closed hearts,
an evening amid the colporteurs who hurl our sad world into
                   cesspools:
    'Whites! Negroes! Bankers! Dead miners recovered!
    Machinery! Mutilated bells of the battlefronts . . .',
    which numb our brain,
an evening which falls from the night and swarms from
                   green,

wrecked hillsides,
from potato wagons,
an evening, which drives you into desolation
among weak limbs,
in blind games of pain,
where the hunger beats the measure for the vices . . .

Under the Mourning Moon

You say nothing because you are too sick to say how potent
        the earth is, which I created in my nights,
the earth of flesh and the earth of
        sun-drenched landscapes,
the earth which squandered not one drop of blood,
        the earth which was unfamiliar to my fathers and which

becomes my message with new instruments,
        when summer comes with searing August
and winter with the roaring of the tree trunks
        between the mountains of this district,
which is worthy of no second god and lives on bread and
                                                        vanity
        ever since those days in which wars were concocted
inside some wrecked brain in the capital.

You say nothing because you are too sick to say how great
        the torment is, which must plough furrows through my
                                                        soul
from morning to evening and through these midnights,
                which no longer feel a blade of grass,
        because your music is too vain
for the butter vats and the coffins of the dead who rise
        from their prisons with the croaking of the frogs
between their breeding seasons.

You say nothing because you are too sick to say how deep
the sea is which my ship plies, how black the backs
of dolphins are which glisten on the reefs of a dream,
which stretches from a thousand faces of the north
to a thousand faces of the south,
which is greater than this earth and mightier
than the November storm which cost the life of my fathers
and umpteen million wagonloads of their days!

You say nothing because your prayer is misheard
and because your flesh shines of sweet rot in the night
and your soul darts through the blue forests
in that time of potato sprouts and May processions!

You say nothing because you are too sick to say who
dreamt of your damnation in those prisons created by
God
in mountain huts and guesthouses, in cellars
where the rats twinkle like stars
because day and night are the music of gravel,
which drinks your sleep
and the conquest of wars,
which you concocted during the raptures of spring!

You say nothing because you are too sick to say what
must be said, what makes these hills so sad
and this sunrise and this toil of the farmers
and this toil of the birds
and this toil which cultivates destruction in every blade, in
every riverbed,
everywhere where hands are over the earth.

In My Capital

I

In my capital I was a do-nothing, a stable boy
   for the prime minister and I saw through the windows
of the Hofburg and thought that I will never reside
   at one of those big desks and never
smoke a cigar behind the blue velvet curtains that once
   spoilt Metternich's view of the green trees.

II

I was driven by strange whips, by books and Bible quotes,
   and the November wind exposed my shanks
and preached angry psalms into my tortured barn-waltz brains.

   I stumbled over the refinements
of these lifeless creatures, who crawled over the GRAVES
   in black and blue suits, flicking cigars
and closing a deal with the cement and vinegar factories.
   I tripped over instruments which a sickly Mozart
tried to bring to life
   and over the pain which sank into those faces
which hurtled along the tramway
   like sad boxes of ashes, a morass of suffocating souls,
who dreamt of honey bread and flocks of swallows,
   of rich pastures and simmering Easter lambs
in fermenting valleys.

I stumbled over the churches whose boy choirs
fed none of the hungry, whose Masses resembled the
                              wreaking of this century
    . . . the same voices, the same trumpet blasts, the same
                            repellent organ pipes . . .

III

In my capital I went to sleep when the day rose
    with its furrowed brow and the milkmen
silently began their day's work, when children started up
    in their dirty tear-stained beds
and fell back once more into the night
    which let their young flesh to lie.
I heard the new mothers groan and I saw golden lamps
    sway in the sweet-smelling park wind,
through which my brain sometimes reeled, when it was
                              shattered
    in this dead body by the Danube.

IV

I came in order to see their prisons and their work,
    their faces and their solitude,
I came because I was nauseated by milk and honey,
    by these brutal liquors of the sky!
I heard of weddings whose tables
    collapsed under the weight of the fruit and
the feast of music . . . of the gala receptions and
philosophies,
    of the libraries and the landmarks of Romans and
                              Greeks . . .

V

But what did I find in my capital?
    Death with its mouth of ashes, destructive, thirst and
                                 hunger,
which to my own hunger was distasteful, for it was
    a hunger for meat and bread, for faces and toilets,
a hunger which stammers the shame of this city,
    a hunger for misery
shimmering from window to window, begetting spring and
                             a foul fame
    beneath the stairway of heaven.
I was trapped and tired of rot,
    far from the forests and far from the death wishes of the
                            mouldering years.
The grey, crumbling stones of these timbers groaned
                            furiously,
    but I was this laughter, the laughter of hell,
this human trap of myself in which I ran,
    trying to forget a blackish hour of the world
in the November wind of my existence . . .

Paris

Your tears for the one who does not want them.

Paul Eluard

    I

I cannot sleep, for the circus is leaving
    outside my window and the people cheer! As though
                  through the grass
of hell I see their faces, the ones who bring to this city
                  destruction
    and inexhaustible poetries of which I have heard
sleeping between Nancy and Versailles,
    from the prison cells under the stars of the river,
which sends its bitterness into the sky,
    on the banks and in woods, which stink of the corpses of
                Germans.
I slept as if I were a shepherd and read my Bible
    and gave no thought to the metro, which dissects my
                sleep,
as if I were too guilty, as if I could have ruined girls
    and seduced young men to sleep through ten hours,
as if I were one of the beggars who do not show their face
    when the sun goes strolling over the cathedral,
as if I were the man with eyes that stab you, for
    I don't want to starve to death, 'à la fin tu es las de ce
              monde ancien . . .'

O, I know my Pascal and my poets of the pavilions,
    the groans from the hospitals above the Seine,
which brings the stinking morning through your window,
                            in the middle
    of your heart, which you must bear even though you
                            would like to eat
this heart in a green, sunlit square, this heart,
    which once crawled into the sweet hay and dreamt of
                            whispering milk pails,
this heart which choked on country roads, which was in
                            factories
    and had to breathe in the sweat of mindless
                            cheesemakers,
this heart, which saw the day break before the sun came,
    which slept among thieves on the cold platforms
at the end of the railroad tracks,
    on the shores of alcohol,
    on the shores of grass,
    on the shores of fame,
    on the shores of science,
this heart, which desires to walk out of prison and be free as
                            a bird
and the March clouds above the Eiffel Tower, with which I
                            alone am
    to carry on the greatest conversations this year,
this year of sorrow.

II

I cannot sleep, for three million make so much noise!
    Three million who dream about the achievements of
                            technology,

who pray in their struggle amid the push rods of locomotives,
 which steam from their glass sarcophagi into the
          morning,
I cannot sleep, for I know they hate my face,
 this face, which was once flesh and blood
and which screws itself into the scowl of the devil on this
          night,
 into the abyss, into the end,
which deserves no peace,
 this my face, which saw more than all the faces of this
         city put together,
this city that weeps in its trees and under the silk dress
 of the chanteuse on the Place de la Concorde . . .

III

If I could say how often I wanted to die in this night,
dying without a psalm and without a mother and father, to
         die suffocated
like cattle driven between walls,
 to die like a crushed worm, without help,
to die like the starling, which is smashed by the wheel of the
         metro overhead,
 to die like the souls of the trees that send their secrets
on the wind to all the oceans when spring comes, for
 'à la fin tu es las de ce monde ancien . . . '
 so much pain, so much stench from the bodies of
      people who I have never before breathed.

IV

I can no longer bear to be as low as the asparagus vendor,
to be as low as the fortune teller and as low
as the priest who stubs his toe on the holy-water basin of
Notre Dame.
I can no longer bear to be as poor as the beggar
who has pocketed my last ten francs
without saying 'bonjour',
poorer than the prostitutes and the children under the
chestnut trees
licking ice cream with the tongues of the devil,
which look like the tongues of this warm, shimmering,
accidental world.
They all have no names, they are not called Spring, not
Summer,
not Winter, they all bear this beautiful name in common,
PARIS,
and peer into the night with their open mouths
and sunken cheeks, silent and gasping from worldly pain,
which taught them the science
with which they could accuse God!
You see them oar homewards in their high heels and
sucking in
the air of the brotherly ocean, setting course
and blowing police whistles,
stretching their legs on rickety cushioned chairs, concealing
their ulcers,
and by the bedside reading verses handed down from
the Bible to little girls
when the last glimmers of the day have enough of the sun.

V

And where is your friend who should explain this poetry to
you,
who spears your sausage from above your plate while
reciting a poem by Baudelaire?

Where is your friend who strolls with you along the river in
a fresh shirt
with scented cuffs, moving like one of the young nobles of
the chateaux along the Loire,
from whose mouths the only words that fall are 'Valèry,
Éluard, Coty,
Ile de France' or 'Notre nature est dans le mouvement . . .'?
Where is your friend who tells you ten times a day how rich
you are,
and who lets his thoughts play by the edge of the pond
in which the French are struck in the face by their glorious
history
where they behave as if the Revolution had only ended
yesterday.
Where is your friend who praises your poverty,
cultivated in some village of rotten, dismembered Austria
by a mother who took only three classes in a country
school
and by a father the north wind drove like a beast through
the entrails
of Scandinavian cold,
fleeing from his failure of a soul?

VI

Paris: a sea that takes you to the bottom, a whiff
      of rooftops, mortuaries, of factories and silk skirts,
an air of iridescent trees and tender, spinning dances,
         the stench of open pissoirs, where forsaken men with
                                             their golden water

write of fates, long forgotten, comforting the heart no more
                                    upon crystalline
tarpaper partitions, imprisoned by dust and the hunger of
                                             the dawn,
which rises with the day, which dries off the eyes under
      the arches of a bridge.
This is the vice of my brain, which is destroyed by a
                              million vocabularies
      and by umpteen millions of consolations extending
                              from the Greeks
to the red and green lights of the intersection,
      this is the place where the earth for me was the
                                    coldest . . .
I cannot sleep, I will never sleep
      because I always see this river and always feel
      the disgust of these brothels, this beauty dying between
                              the trunks of the trees
      down the down the Avenue de Ternes . . .
I cannot sleep, for the circus is leaving
      outside my window and the people cheer! I want to
                              forget them all,
for my hunger is enormous . . . it drives me back into a
                                    country,

which no one has ever seen, into a greener country, a
                                        sobbing dawn,
into a country that bears my name,
    a morning without devastation . . .

Venice

From the rotting fish,
from the rotting cats,
amid the squashed summer fruit
your fame waxes:

Maria della Salute, Ca' d'Oro,
Colleoni, Palazzo Ducale . . .

I count my coins on the steps,
lay my ham slice on this dry bread,
and recall to myself the Giorgione
with those gnawed shreds of clouds,
bearing the title,
        'La Tempesta'.

Chioggia

From four thousand years
    we came home,
The lagoon's wine
    dried away in our eyes.
We saw the ships come to an end
    in the rusty evening light,
yet after those ships the children
    did not see us.

      They have never loved the soil
        and the bread,
      silently around their beds there mourns
        the shit of four thousand years.

We witnessed the fish that would not die
    and saw so much agony,
we heard no groans and cries
    from the hospital,
we found the windows open
    to the sea,
from the islands the wind carried
    the shadows of the dead here . . .

      But outside the world waited
        behind the white gate,

above the cypress branches
　　its milky smoke rose upwards.
Only the ribs of boats shown
　　back beneath the moon,
and women bowed before the nets
　　so as to bring luck.

Here they know how to live yet
　　on a day in April,
and when they die before noon
　　they die quietly,
and the market in this famed fishing village
　　is today too
a feast day for all—
　　they bring olive trees in the house
and serve the eel
　　on white tables.

　　They carry honey in black jars
　　　　and they tell of schools of tuna
　　from behind brick walls,
　　　　through a narrow crack—
　　with the cats
　　　　and with the fish they grow old,
　　and they stitch their pain
　　　　on the shore into shawls,

and their evening reeks of fish,
　　and their grave-marker is of stone.
They hoist the sand from the barges

and lie in the boat at night,
and they live by their work,
and many are already dead . . .

From four thousand years
we came home,
The lagoon's wine
dried away in our eyes,
we saw the ships coming to an end
in the rusty evening light,
yet after those ships the children
did not see us.

Below Lies the City

Below lies the city,
    you need not come back,
for its corpse is strewn with flowers.

Tomorrow the river speaks.
    The mountains are in a haze,
although spring comes too late. ˇ

Below lies the city.
    You do not recall names.
From the forests flows the black wine.

And the night falls silent.
    The sick birds came.
And you only stop in mourning.

The Night Which
Pierces My Heart

Sadness

The mountains are red and my brethren walk in my brain
as though Jesus had not been crucified under the stars,
which have no fear of the cruelties of my soul, which I
have buried in a valley, as though I had not been born, back
                                                    then,
in April, in that angry month, which washes the stones
to gravestones, where perch the consorts of my loneliness,
with their pale faces, and the storm gouges their eyes out
under the distant moon.

Why these days, why the dying,
why all of this, what I do not love, not the bush
and not the blossoms in the mouth of the ass and not the
                                                    cry
of my limbs in the autumn and not the toil of the farmers
and none of the glory of pain, which my mother burdened
                        me with when she had to die
among the besotted brewmasters at the edge of the lake,
                            which gorges on my dead
under the laughter of the stars.

I did nothing which could spoil your bliss, nothing
but write a few verses, which brought my brother to tears,
which made my sister—with the blossoms of the March
                        wind—jealous, I ate nothing

which you missed from your table, drank nothing which
                                    reeks of your weddings and
the ballad of the granaries in which I can no longer return
                                                    because
I sounded the false bells on the bank of the river, which
                                                offers my sadness
to the empty skulls of immortality
every day, from one morning to another, soundless, as if I
                                    were turning to ash before
I awoke in the spring flesh of these cities.

What I think when I see the empty streets, the windows of
                                            men and women
who drank so much decay, such that God must protect you,
who cut your green and your grey and the black of the
                                            river into pieces,
who did not praise your hunger and the sadness of your
                                                        nights,
during which you perished amid every stone and every toad
into oblivion! In oblivion! In that despair
of roots!

I no longer see a face which I could love, no flesh
which would bring my desire pleasure and no death
which would satisfy my being alone . . . The fields are empty!
                                                The houses
are violet with candles! Their doors creak their contempt in
                                            your tribulation, when
you come home and every rotting mouth which owns a field,
an apple tree, a milk cow, some grass,
curses you . . .

And when you want to go away, you have no idea where!
And when you want to drink water, you stand in the desert!
And when you want to beg, the filth of their riches chokes
you!
And when you look for your grave, they bring you a dishful
of beauty!

. . . I no longer see a face . . . Only the black crumbling clay
of their afflictions and the anger that turns their life into dust.

Biography of Pain

Where I slept yesterday is today a day of rest. Outside the
                                                    entrance
chairs are stacked on top of each other and no one, when I
ask about myself, has seen me.
The birds are fluttering upwards to mark my face in the
                                                    clouds
over my house and over the garden of the dead.

I have conversed with the dead and spoken of that guitar of
                                                    the world,
which their mouths no longer produce and their lips,
which speak a language that distresses my cousin's dog.

The earth speaks a language which no one understands,
for it is inexhaustible—I have drawn stars and pus from it in
                                                    despair
and have drunk wine from its jug
which is distilled from my pain.

These roads lead to banishment. I hear God
behind a glass pane and the Devil in a shouting match
and together both reach for my heart which proclaimed the
                                                    downfall of souls.

The leaves in the streets whirled incessantly
and brought about destruction amid the tombstones.
I would like to dream of the green in October.
Underneath the front door is posted a commandment, the
                                        commandment:
          THOU SHALT NOT KILL
— — — but every day in the newspaper there are three
                                        murders,
which could be mine or one of my friends.
I read it like a fable,
about a stab wound to another—without ever getting bored.
And while they confuse flesh and fame, my soul sleeps
under the wave of God's hand.

Torment

I die from the sun and
from the wind and from the children who bicker over the
         dog, I die
on a morning which will come to no poem; just sad and
        green and endless
is this morning . . . Father and Mother stand upon the bridge
        and believe
I am coming from the city and bring me nothing
but their mouldering springs in great baskets, and they see
        me—
and they do not see me, for
I die from the sun.

One of these days I will no longer see the bushes, and the
        grass
will take on my sister's grief. The archway
will be black and the sky no longer
out of reach
for my despair . . . One day
I will see everything and blot out the eyes of many
in the early morning . . .

Then I am amid the jasmine again and
watch the gardener as he tidies up the dead in their beds . . .

I die from the sun.—
I am sad, for there will always be days that will not come
any more . . . anywhere.

In a Rug of Water

In a rug of water
I stitch my days,
my gods and my illnesses.

In a rug of green
I stitch my red sorrows,
my blue mornings,
my yellow villages and honey cakes.

In a rug of earth
I stitch my transience.
I stitch in my night
and my hunger,
my sorrow
and that warship of my despair,
sailing over a thousand bodies of water,
into the waters of turmoil,
into the waters of immortality.

The Night

The night trembles before the window, it wants to pierce
                                                    my heart
and call the names which I have shamed.
O, these names which are carved into each cross and which
                                        soil my day's work.
I know, I will get up and destroy my bed
and with that bed the dreams which grew in my hair for
                                            seventy years.

I will get up and recite my verse below
for the beggars who survive on loneliness,
on the streets of transactions. On the streets
where the women cheat their flesh for a day at the fair.
These streets which are made from the wheat of my father
and the poverty of my mother,
who sliced up her arm with a scythe and so looked
like the sun itself.—

O, the night piercing my heart
with all those I have shamed . . .

You Know Nothing, My Brother, of the Night

You know nothing, my brother, of the night,
nothing of this torment which exhausts me
like the poetry which bears my soul,
nothing of these thousand twilights, these thousand mirrors
which will hurl me into the abyss.
You know nothing, my brother, of the night
which I must wade through like a river
whose souls are long choked down by the seas,
and you know nothing of the magic charm,
mine which opened our moon like spring fruit
between the withered branches.
You know nothing, my brother, of the night
which drives me through my father's graves,
which drives me through woods greater than the earth,
which teaches me to see the suns rise and fall
in those sickly glooms of my day's work.
You know nothing, my brother, of the night,
of the turmoil racking the mortar,
nothing of Shakespeare and the white skull
holding umpteen millions of ashes like a stone,
which rolled down the white seacoasts,
laughing over war and decay.
You know nothing, my brother, of the night,

for your sleep walked through the weary tree trunks
of this autumn, through the wind which washed your feet
with snow.

What Drives the Souls through the Lilacs

What drives the souls through the lilacs,
the wind from the forests carrying its catchphrases over the
white
surface of the lake, which carves the faces of centuries' old
pain
in the prison cells of farmers and monks,
where thousands perish and boast the music of birds
for their achievements and the noiseless movement
of departed animals which flee into the dark of the mine,
the world changing into a hell whipped by the rain?

What drives the souls through the lilacs
on this morning, where no one finds a house any more
and none of the gardens shine by the marker stones of poetry,
where the mortar of old grey walls trickles away
before the forests which border this ode for a time that is
no longer ours?
They find no more pebbles for their agony
and for the agony of the father and mother.
One morning their nurse will see them
with the eyes of the night . . .

What drives the souls through the lilacs,
which cast a spell over this cruel earth by eight o'clock,

                when the hearse
with the new mother rolls crunching over the white gravel,
into heaven under cedars and poplars . . . and minutes later
children with their book bags rush outdoors to school
and people the green earth with their screams,
which wake up the dead and cause the old hospital orderly
                                 to unleash
his breakfast barrage of abuse at the spring . . .?

What drives the souls through the lilacs
when the mist of blood rises through the gardens
and the hillsides breathe heavily amid the green flesh of
                            awakening days,
whose affliction floats sluggishly in the river with soft
                                 laments,
where the girls of the lyceum hate their black dresses
and the white bows in their pigtails
and silently march behind the suffocating apparition of the
                         nuns into the soil
ever higher up that hill, to the chapel,
to sing an old psalm?

What drives the souls through the lilacs,
that cry, which escaped in sleep, these syllables of blackness,
the sickness and the thirst of sly murderers
who strangle the dream between the apple trees
and the distant shadow of the city
which pounds death with the shadows of the spring,
which loves their frenzy with a thousand spectral suns,
with millions of mouths and eyes going up in a fire,

into the stirring spectacle of nothing, when that weeping
                                                    wound of days
blankets any thoughts of pears and rivers, children and sad
                                                    old men?

Throes

I will cross over and cry, loudly
cry and call to my father and extract a
confession, standing in the fire
and sticking my burning hands
into the jaws of the snow.

I will run home flowers from the fields
and break the branches of my bushes for the throes of death.
I will give my grief a letter and commend it to God
and tell it that it is a life like no life,
Grief in the twilight of those cities of our fathers!

I will cross over and proclaim from where I come
and where I go.
I go as far as it takes until no one can overtake me any more
with dirty shoes. No cold will freeze my heart to stone
before the uncertainty of beclouded gods!

Limbo

I have seen You like someone drowning
  open-mouthed
  about the world.
I have seen You,
  but across the bridge is a cloud which does not last,
  such that we sell our house and set fire to our heart
  for one day at the fair and watch the way the raven
                                        devours its meat,
  and the cow tramples through its own filth.
I have seen You,
  Your face is the face of Hell.
I have seen You,
  Your feet walk through my forests and bring torment.
  Your voice flees through my rooms.
I have seen You,
  Your blood makes me sick: my hair moulders under the
                                        earth,
  under the wonderful earth
  smelling of the grass of ill-fated steppes.

Ash Wednesday

I would like to walk out
    after the night
and cleanse my hands and my
    lips,
I would like to cleanse myself
    in the sun and
in the grass—

    But it's raining
and my grass
    is brown
and old—

Nine Psalms

('God's soul is in fishermen'.)

I

I want to be angry,
I want to forget everything,
I want to forget the mouth of the fish,
for the mouth of the fish is dark.
I want my struggle said in prayer,
the great struggle for my soul.
For I am poor.
I am a pauper in the night.
Everyone has forgotten me,
even though I see the table
and the wine which I will drink.
It is the wine of God,
that black wine for my red brain,
which I will drink in the night,
in the night burning my feet,
which fills my land and the sea,
the night of the cheated,
the night of glowing apple trees,
the night of fountains,
the night of ballad singers,
the night which tramples my snake's head,
the night of the clever,

the night of fish.
I will drink it.
I want to drink it angry
in the night of my utter poverty.

      II

Each night my path leads into the gravel pit,
down into the gravel pit of my despair,
in the rubble,
in the bitterness
that makes my eyes powerless.
I hear in the stones
the fury of the wind
which turns my wretched children into dust.
Lord,
my cursed name,
the cursed name of my children
is moaning in the stones.
But You are this unending rain of grief,
the unremitting rain of desolation.
the rain of stars.
The rain of the weak
which makes my eyes powerless.

      III

What I do is badly done.
What I sing is badly sung,
which is why You have a right
to my hands
and my voice.

I will work to my ability.
I promise You the harvest.
I will sing the song of a lost people.
I will sing of my people.
I will love.
Even criminals!

With criminals and the defenceless
I will establish a new homeplace
—despite what I do is badly done,
what I sing is badly sung.
That is why You have a right
to my hands,
to my voice.

IV

I will go to the edge,
to the edge of the earth
and taste eternity.
I will fill my hands with earth
and speak my words,
the words that turn to stone on my tongue
to build God up once more,
the great God,
the only God,
the father of my children,
at the edge of the earth,
the ancient father,
at the edge of the earth,
in the name of my children.

V

Let me see
every fish in the sea
and all the children of the earth
and taste the smell of the morning
and the smell of the evening.
I want to hear the language of the fish
and the language of the wind
which is like the language of the angels.
I want to hear the voice
of ephemeralness!
Every voices is the voice of ephemeralness.
Every voice that ever was heard.
All sing of ephemeralness.
You sing of ephemeralness too.

VI

The evening sends me grain from the tombs,
the velvet taste of peace
and the dew of beggardom.
O, all these beggars on the earth!
I see them walk across the grass
in the Christmas of ponds,
in the spring of prayers,
Let me see this spring,
the millions of beggars on the earth,
before it is too late!

VII

I could say what must be said
as my body turns into the greatest trap of my life,
my innocence into the greatest guilt!
I could say who I am—
behind the welded doors,
behind my proud memory,
I could say, as the struggle against laws
(against vile laws)
goes on inside me,
as the fire of my flesh burns my soul,
I could say what I am given to say,
the hell of my blood,
the blackness in my eyes,
the unfruitfulness of my songs,
to tell of poverty!
The enormous poverty which humbled me.
The enormous poverty which perfected me.
The poverty which split me apart
for this perfection!

VIII

Black is the grass, Father,
black is the earth,
black are my thoughts
for I am a poor person.
Black is the earth,
black is the sunset,
black is my message.

Black is the coat that I will not take off any more,
black are the stars of my passage,
black are the thoughts of my dying.
Where I found this black, this eloquence-despising black?

IX

I fear myself no more.
I am no longer afraid
of what will come.
My hunger is sated,
my suffering is drained,
my dying makes me happy.
I carry my fish
up the mountain.
Everything is in the fish,
what I leave behind.
In the fish is my grief,—
and my failure is in the fish.
I will say
how glorious the earth is when I arrive,
how glorious the earth is . . .
Without having to fear myself . . .
I expect
that the Lord expects me.

Death and Thyme

Summer Rain

Give up, you birds,
        no evening
gives me comfort, across
        the bridge rain falls
in my sorrow, no rustling
        of summer
changes me,
        no wind
keeps me awake . . .

        Tomorrow morning
I will not walk under
        the trees,
my lids are heavy with sleep
        after winter and snow,
I want to retreat
        in the rain
to leaves
        and dark coffins.

Give up, you birds, I freeze,
        my shadow
waxes across
        the night

in the woods,
    there rest,
the dead
    under black blossoms,
the wandering dead.

Before Bryant's Fame

I lived long in the forests and on the graves,
and I was a witness when the sun came for the first time
                                             and lay
by a girl already at the forest's edge, sleeping, more
turned towards the earth than all the stars . . . I was long
                                                  there
when Shakespeare died and Bryant's fame
withered away in a rotten valley.

Who summoned me in the cities, let that horror
up and climb into my brain, giving birth to my desolate
                                                  heart,
which I already crushed on a fence post
for a thousand years, one in this disgusting earth, and who
                                             was it who bore
me into this land which put up with my father's wrath
as though it were some old man's sorry news?

I often think that I sang these songs too late and overlooked
the morning too late too, the stones of my village that are
against my spirit and my vanity! You know them. Have I not
overrun these poems with vanity and every stall in which
my brothers bellow, empty, full of delusion in beautiful nights,
which I had no love for myself?

I lived long ago, yet I do not know how to tell where I first
buried my flesh and brought tired mothers lies, sick sisters
songs . . . I lacked any grief in ripened lands
and seas, I hardly felt anything save the wind, the wind
                                        as jubilation,
which required my decay, which took a thousand years to
                                        disintegrate.—
        Not for one day
was I alone, so much was I in decay . . . long before Bryant's
                                        fame
and long before Shakespeare,
        close to the earth.

Black Hills

I was, for one lives only once, in Italy,
I have seen France, the terraces of princes in Provence,
famous paintings and secluded lakes
and the enormous strain in the lives
of the farmers on the hillsides of Dalmatia; also
I am no stranger to the lot of the knitter on the steps of the
                                        Alipasha Mosque
in Sarajevo; wine, olives, the foul stench of a ship's hold
put me to sleep, also
I drove an ass and ate cheese that must be ground with a flat
                                        stone.
I fed children on the Rialto Bridge. I came
for dying, my song went undefeated, still
the foulness of my thoughts lifted me.
I drank with the devastated fishermen and partook
of their strength;
the day retreated and inscribed
its affliction on the black hills, such that I shivered.

For a long time I have seldom felt homesick, neither
people nor towers moved me, even
the forests kept to being forests in my mind and no house
over the mountains let me leave the world, the one that I
                                        invented, as someone unique.

'The sea is vast, the deserts inexhaustible too,
        and is it better not to suffer far from such places . . .'?
I can't depend on my tavern for very long any more.
Father, Mother simply exist as temples. The world, which
I invented, nourishes me
as long as the verses and the scraps of meat
deal with bread and return, wine and fruitfulness.

Living and Dead

The souls will not return, those the frost
    disturbed under the slow path
of the snow, which drove its hours
    for their fates, waking the dead as it did
along the bank of the raging river.
    Tomorrow my father will bring home
the first branches from the journey and many
    will sing a hymn of mourning for him,
a hymn of mountains, lakes and shadows
    which flee the ice-cold night, when October
inscribes its vast verses across the hillsides
    about the dead and the living, of the earth
which brings to the singular one glory
    and the villages the pain of millennia.
The souls will not return, those the wind
    drove east through the forests, where my mother
plucked her life from a rotted tree
    which held no forty-sixth summer . . .
They will be sombre and no one will recognize
    them like sisters, no one will see
the moon as Father staggering home between the trees
    at midnight.
They will only speak of homesickness
    and perish in the defile of their days, between a tree
                                                    trunk

and the hiding place of a tired blackbird.

    No November will come when we
speak of our dead who see their fame
    rotting away in the earth. Tomorrow
the sea will praise the dead, and this century,
    the century of our children,
will be forgotten.
The souls will not return who flee
    during the failing day into the deep twilight of autumn,
into the night of prisons.

    Outside my window, where the well-pole caws,
grass will remain at the foot of the hill
    which conceals its history: the history
of apple blossoms and death
    which lingered on cold days
as it cherished the sunrise
    and the hungry words of that millwheel which
      becomes
the night and the river to catastrophe.

With the Shadows of the Crows

With the shadows of the crows, the dead emerge in the
                                        farmland,
beginning a game which deals with the mothers and sisters
of this sad earth, whom I still heard in the forest yesterday
                                        and by the river
incanting their devastating spells in the twilight.

With the shadows of the crows, the dead emerge from the
                                        pride
of the green mountains, which had been the last refuge of
                                        my father
when the war drove its martyr's stakes into April,
which afflicted the tender spring with its icy wind . . .

With the shadows of the crows, the dead rise up and walk
through the desolate villages peopled by butchers, priests
and brutal souls; through the muddy cemetery, whose grass
sings a hymn of the sensitive earth striking the red face of
                                        the sun.

With the shadows of the crows, the dead plunge back into
                                        the night,
leaving behind the fame of the ballad singers and Sunday's
                                        torments,

the forgotten stones on the furrowed face of this earth,
which will speak through the cherry trees in a thousand
years.

Beyond the Wheat

Beyond the wheat the warriors of this century die,
which passed through my country while April
kindled a fire for the lost souls.
In grey sunflowers, I rouse the music of the silence,
which gives my attainments new fame and my grief
this torn-up picture of cities which are of stone and ash—
Corpse after corpse lies behind their weapons
which glint in the morning air before this sinking time.
Tomorrow my fame goes down in the streams!
                              Tomorrow awakens
the protests of my flesh at the edges of the forests, flesh which
is stabbed by ten thousand knives and more; the fragrance
                              of the apples,
which rot in the churchyards of this landscape, penetrates
amid the music of my battered skulls, which offer no peace,
before the snow starts falling and the earth becomes brown
from the feet of the ruined. Tomorrow my silence
will plant trees on new hills, whose black grass
will go up in bright flames. How sad will this land be,
this motherly land facing the mountains, which I let follow
                              me
after those days of the sea, those days of fish and those days
                              of cities,

after the dinner music, which the gods of the ponds provided
                    for my opus of annihilation
with its flowers and knives, rotting flesh and wing beats.
When I was born so much sadness was still in the world,
and the earth was bright with the ships of ghosts, who
wrote green verses and planted dreams in hothouses,
who brought forth new souls in the houses of joy! This time
                    is no more to see.—
A wretched marketplace spews its everyday hymns
in my despair and flattens the hills and the dead
who are walking through the waters, through the waters of
                    the drunks,
where faces meet at the feast of the world. Grey
and old are how the girls look today, those who brought us
                    bread
and lit fires before the open doors and who sang their songs
    to the night (which stifled the temple)
while the moon hung in wet branches, freezing as
the pain of the world came and went with it . . . Never
                    again
will come those early fears, never again that day which
                    blossomed in blue faces,
never again that night which whittled away its heart under
                    the chestnut tree and
let the split pieces fall in my dream. I will go forth
and forget these solitary houses, the people
and pigsties on the shore of the lake and the black tracks of
                    the tanks
which tied up the fields, the grain, the wheat,
of these people with their desire for heaven past praying for!
                    Never again

do the dull moans of the cattle track reach me and the
                         clatter of January's hoofs
which slip into the valley . . . With morning drops of dew
                         will fall
and tear apart the web which preaches the vices.
The streets will descend into this life deserted: into hideous
                         things!
Tomorrow everything is different! Tomorrow the flowers
        know nothing more of the evening wind! And of
the splashing of the millstream! Tomorrow is June! Or
                         November? Tomorrow
is the going down which leads to the islands, which are
                         allotted to my soul . . .
and my storms!

Tired

I am tired . . .
With the trees I held a conversation.
With the sheep I suffered the drought.
With the birds I sang in the woods.
I loved girls in the village.
I gazed up at the sun.
I saw the sea.
I worked with the potter.
I swallowed dust on the country road.
I saw the flowers of melancholy in my father's field.
I saw death in the eyes of my friends.
I extended my hand to the souls of the drowned.
I am tired . . .

At Twenty-Six

Twenty-six years
of the forests, the fame and the poverty,
twenty-six New Year's Days and no friend
and death
and always the sun again
and no pair of waterproof shoes for the tremors of the earth.
Twenty-six years
like a dream, a badly sung chorale
amid the wind in April,
and no house and no mother
and no conception of God, of the father who speaks from
                                        the day labourers.
Twenty-six years
among beer drinkers, saints, murderers and madmen
in the city and in the engorged villages,
created daily and daily spit out,
staggering from Christmas to Christmas,
no shoemaker, no innkeeper, no beggar,
without a guitar and without a Bible,
homesick in October,
deathly ill of flowers in August.
Twenty-six years,
which no one has experienced,
no child, no grave and no

gravediggers with whom I can talk at the beer table.
Twenty-six years
in a rare unwarrantedness against all,
of being drunk amid the cider barrels of my father,
in rotten valleys
dissipated and deserted in laughter,
nothing but snow and utter darkness
and those deep tracks of forefathers,
which my deadly soul retrudges.

Where the Last Breath of March Wind Is Felt

We seek the dead
under the grass and spread fingers
and have no rest, not tomorrow and the day after
and under the tree and beyond the hills
and across the desolate gorge,
where the last breath of March wind is felt.

Before we often complained to the old man
and despised these children,
our mother did not understand and our father,
and tomorrow and the day after, in a thousand years
we will ask who has died there
in the dark.

We seek the dead,
we drink fever from black mugs,
we dream of the moon and the stars
and drink and endure grief,
and drive horses and tie up sacks
and build caskets and go to sleep.

We seek the dead
under the grass and spread fingers

and find no rest, not tomorrow and the day after
and under the tree and beyond the hills
and across the desolate gorge,
where the last breath of March wind is felt.

Spring of Black Flowers

Spring of black flowers, you are driven
by the dead's fever,
Spring of black flowers, you are driven
by an endless wind from the north,
my April is a grave,
a sinister dream night of black flowers,
you are driven by weird sisters into the land,
when the crows shriek
and the hills drink showers.

Spring of black flowers, you are driven
by the dead's fever,
Spring of black flowers, you are driven
by an endless wind from the north,
I will sleep, tomorrow
the snow and solitude will already cover me following your
                                                        shoes . . .
you are driven by weird sisters into the land,
when the crows shriek
and the hills drink showers.

The Wind Blowing Spoke to These Fields

The wind blowing spoke to these fields:
Corpses came from deserted taverns,
Piled meat high before the deep, black forests,
drank the ordeal of their last days
in scorched, desolate summer valleys,

for the days of mourning follow from grief.
Those not loved were soon forgotten,
but they tended to their wreaths
and went through umpteen thousand earthen mugs
in the celebrations of their fatigue.

They were preserved from the night too,
by morning their feet made tracks
in the clay of the dead city;
outside the apple trees blossomed late,
the stalks danced and the wind from the east
said nothing of another world.

Those days no longer come around,
not from these villages, these cities.
Many islands bear their names.
But with evening their mourning is seen
drifting home between the play of clouds.

Autumn

You will come back tomorrow,
bakers, tailors, liars,
streetsweepers
jealous of my song
which my battered soul sings.

You will come back tomorrow,
you birds, you trees, you wonderful
prison cell of summer
which my father sent
from the black mountains.

You will come back tomorrow,
those who write my fame in the earth
beneath the red chestnuts,
and those who despise my work and my blood,
that of the world
in autumn.

You will come back tomorrow,
dead friends and faded dreams,—
you hear a blackbird, your shadow
runs through the riverbed,
and nothing, no one at all
will give you comfort.

Death and Thyme

The earth reeked of thyme and death,
    of hay and wind,
from the stream my mother's soul climbed
    and went above the trees as in those days
of cloudless, bitter springs.
    The earth smelt of thyme and death
and no one came with a basket
    to carry them home.—
Since the pig cost too much,
    they carried home no earth,
not the earth which reeked of death and thyme.
    Through the oaks I looked
    down into the village.
I heard the church fair's trumpets
    and the trombones of smoked ham,
and I heard the sausages crack
    and the boards of the dance floor
in the laughter of the priest.—
    Upon a stone,
I slept for a thousand years.
    No one came for a piece of the earth
which reeked of death and thyme.

Letter to My Mother

You come in the night, when the maidservant bares her
                                                    breasts
    and the apple tree is empty
    and the stars destroy my name.
You come when the stream stops to mourn and its words
    freeze in my window
    and the sheep flee from my laughter to the corner of
                                                    the stall,
You come when the centre of the world
    spits a stream of blood with a sigh,
You come when the field is barren and the eyes
    of fish glow green,
You come when no one comes, when the girl who gave me
                                                    her breasts
    hides from my fame,
    when she let her hair glisten in the moonlight like a
                                                    millions of years,
You come when they hit me without ever knowing my
                                                    prayer,
    which I will say with these opening words: 'I am
    driven by the gloom . . .'
You always come when I am tired. I pay you
    back for my life with a fear
    falling apart on your absurd gravestone
    over the enormous lie of autumn.

Who Are Dead Now

Who are dead come carousing now, such that
your mouth waters and the earth looks
vile to you, which does not let you feel
wine and summer and sweet flesh,
the wonderful cellars of the ones rotting,
who overshadow their graves unabated,
when the watchdogs are not baying at the forest.

Up from foul trenches as though from the hells
of the forefathers, buried, buried and dulled
with grief, the dead members of mankind
shout in the night, but their bodies were
long rotted from the good fortune of dying and
lacking finery, for they were decked out by their outfitters
and hardly satisfied by the sea and their vileness.

How the stones fell upon their arms, those who
lived for joy and for merriment and full
cups of wake dinners—a music of radiant skeletons
and a hunger for transience drove them like an army
of mouldering summers through sombre paths,
and from the valleys we heard the sounds
of the mute warriors who had fallen
for a stone, for a prick and a whore.

Their paths are so deep that you do not walk through them
and cannot demolish them with the laughter
of princes and women of the earth in labour,
and their thighs sound like music in misery's stalls,
those that deliver the dull wrath of beasts
to your agony. Betrayal, betrayal, O the bitter impermanence
of spring following grey, well-trodden hoofs,
where no waxing of the gloom drives you across the
                                                              mountains.

I have seen them in the winter, and see them to this day
on their feet bearing melancholy and black sorrow,
down into the cities, the torn-up plazas, over which a
                                                summer wind
fares in its purity, into sick valleys which stretch with wet
                                                                    grass
into the sky, into the world, into harbours, utter darkness,
                                                fields whose seed
stinks of people after the skies burst; moments
like moss which recedes into oblivion under the moon, into
the day's work of a bricklayer or a potter.

During the night no one spoke of islands and no one paid
when innkeepers forced their slab of speck on you, the
                                                poetry
of hospitality, heaped across the river and from much honey
                                                and much
hunger smelling of the dreamt earth in a world which
resembles your own save in the entrails; they spoke not
of the hundreds of houses, graves, hills, bridges, which
were your sorrow, not of beauty—but they boasted all,

and their temples sunk unabated and without peace
into oblivion, in shit and water, black, which no one loved.

Return to Love

Yeats Was Not There

(The Irish poet William Butler Yeats often glorified the
return to the rural home place in his verse.)

My name
    The fields do not accept,
the meadows send my life
    back to cities and towns;
the trees withdraw their roots,
    the streams are close-mouthed
when in the village
    I go to the grave of my mother.
No one gives me a cup and says
    I should drink from it,
no one opens his bed
    for me.
If they knew how
    I freeze!
In the forests and
    behind the house
they accuse me of lies.

Return to Love

The mountains approached and spoke only of dying
and the many dead escorted a blackbird and remained mute
all the way down into the inescapable cities ...
... only the millwheel worried, worried as though these
                                                waters were
lonelier still as you saw her once more in these rooms where
the smell of the grain mingled with her fantasies.

Why did I come here? I almost didn't see how I was
                                        devouring my own flesh.
Her I often called ... Was it from the south? Was it
from a cold country? Was it a voice that
my fatherland regarded with contempt?
I know no happiness which is more faraway than this love.

Birds blackened the winter passages of my loneliness
and brought news of deserted brothels, of wine
and of child corpses, those of grief—through my nights went
                                                their footsteps.
The snow followed me with its obliterating poetry.

Before the Apple Tree

I am not dying until I have seen the cow
    in my father's stall,
until the grass stops making my tongue sour
    and the milk changes my life.
I am not dying until my cup is filled to the brim
    and the love of my sister reminds me
of how our valley is beautiful,
    where they knead butter
and slice symbols in the slab of speck for Easter . . .
    I am not dying until the forest sends its storms
and the trees talk of summer,
    until my mother walks on the road with a red scarf
behind a jerking wheelbarrow in which she pushes
    her good fortune: apples, pears, hens and straw—
I am not dying until the door shuts, through
    which I came
before the apple tree—

I Must Go Back into the Village

I must go back into the village, where I grew up,
    along the river which washes my graves,
in the soul of the house in which my father bred
    wine grapes and the life of his children,
where it is carved in tuffstone: 'Hit that cider and funeral
                        ham.'
    I must go back into the village, where they smeared me
                  with their catchphrases
in the night which tastes of the hay of hunger,
    in the shadows which devoured the hills,
in the gloom of blocks of thought on which my name is
                stands, the name of my remains.
    I must go back into the village that mistreated my
                    homesickness,
in which they whisked milk into water,
    in which they destroyed my stars with their laughter.
I must go back into the village in which
    the shoes of my father are erased,
in which my mother starved during the last year of the war,
    in which the fish glowed as the only sky!
I must go back into the village where the oats are like the
                sun,

    where the cows go,
where the streams presage the lovely way fear is before cities,

where the cup is filled with dew and envy.
I must go back into this village
    before I am dead
and eaten away by the wind which bears my mark.

The Wind

The wind comes in the night
    and carries me back into the villages,
into the dull swish-swash of the butter troughs.

The wind comes in the night,
    it spins my name in chestnut leaves
and drives it back north.

The wind comes in the night,
    before the face of the sun
which abducted my brother.

The wind comes in the night,
    its cry of pain swirls
in countless treetops,

that cry which my father did not know,
    the wind, the wind, the wind

    which gathers the dead,
which flings open the front doors,
    that drives my soul,

the wind, the wind, the wind.

At Night the Scent of the Bushes Returns

At night the scent of the bushes returns.
The souls dart from black rooms.
But we sleep and dream and do not know,
was that Father? Was that Mother?
Was that the springtime which passed?

At night stars hang like drops of blood.
The river water digs into the graves.
But we sleep and dream and do not know,
was that Father? Was that Mother?

At night a dead man stands at the field's edge.
He is coming for wine and bitter bread.
But we sleep and dream and do not know,
was that Father? Was that Mother?
Was that the springtime which passed?

At night the fishermen walk with wet nets
beyond the sea in a sad land.
But we sleep and dream and do not know,
was that Father? Was that Mother?

Before the Village

The faces, which emerge from the field, ask
    me about coming back.
My cry does not disturb the swallow
    which perches on the broken branch. Black
is my soul, which the wind blows
    on the sea, reeking of the salt of the earth.
My legend is mortal.
    Under that tree, which is like my brother,
I count the stars of mariners.

At the Well

The moon peers from the well.
    Who will
bring its eyes home for the winter,
    when the snow blankets the earth?
    Who will
speak my name, see those flowers again
    which the rain drives?
    Who will
console me when the souls of the trees
    petrify in a thousand years?
    Who will
erect a gravestone for my desolation,
    and not ask about my world?
    Who will
love those birds, which I despise,
    for they fly south.

Death

Death has beaten me into the summer hay.
    Now it hangs around outside and laughs
and chokes the pear tree.
    No one shakes it down,
no trumpet blast
    scares it away into the hills,
from the valleys they come, those who will slay me,
    farmers, merchants, butchers
and that priest with the Easter lamb
    entrusted to my care.
Death has beaten me into the summer hay.
    No one breaks
my fame in two for me and lets me go . . .

Altentann

The day takes off his shirt.
    Naked, he climbs into the garden bed
and calls the birds together.
    In the black puddles
his red face cowers,
    which the farmers have battered.
The grass jabs my brain
    with spears of shadows—

In the neighbour's window
    sits a bird
as the keeper of my thoughts
    until this rude sleep
pulls off my wet shoes.

My Heart Is in the Wheat

My heart is in the wheat, red
    like the land,
beautiful and mad like the earth,
    which kills me.

I see Father in the east
    young, with red scarf
and bare feet
    walking across my homesickness.

I see my mother standing at my grave
    old and frail,
the blood drips
    from her cheek
into my ephemeralness.

Parents' House

They are not here any more,
    other phrases guide me down
to meat and wine,
    other words drive me
into their deserted rooms,
    only wind goes up to the grinding gate,
the speck and silence
    are all that remain,
and every verse they spoke through the long night
    rots in another land
beyond these mountains,
    where the early morning's strange spell
drives the farmers to drink.
    They are not here any more,
I am freezing like the baker's dog
    brushing its tail along the wall,
I am freezing and cannot
    sleep any more.
My eyelids are as dried up
    as a riverbed in the grey summer
shifting its lament
    down to the sea.
They are not here any more,
    I would like to sleep

and dream of them, those who gave
    me flesh and memory,
the black lifetime,
    the hunger of tragic minds,
and the weary smell of the forests
    and the corrupt fame of the world.
I want to sleep now
    and see their graves.

My Father

My father suffered the dryness of the earth
like the crumbling face of summer,
he climbed up the mountain and rested above the ponds.
This was when our ships sailed against the west.
Never will I forget how Father's hand
grasped for the human soul—
He climbed up the mountain to see that land which they
trampled in seven weeks.
'I tell you,' he said, 'love is indestructible—'
Then the tanks rolled across the wheat field and buried
the hope for the coming year.
They all suffered the dryness of the earth, many
retreated into the night, they said: We
find no stanza in this monstrous verse.
My father believed this earth heard him, for he had
bought himself a hundred acres and a cottage with
an orchard; therein he slept
but found no dream.
He saw a hundred million years in the eyes of the beasts
which flickered on Christmas.
He said: 'We need no candles!'
My father broke the branch from the olive tree and offered
                                                    snow
to the lips of his sisters.

In Siberia he embarked on the journey, yet
he needed an eternity, for they all suffered
the dryness of the earth,
and a voice said inside him: 'I will plunge my light
into human snow.'

My Feet Take Me into the Cemetery

My feet take me into the cemetery,
a thousand years into the cemetery,
into the earth which reeks of the mortar of ghosts,
of the fingers of gypsies.
Into the cemetery my feet take me,
a thousand years into the cemetery,
into the wind,
into the voices of the earth.
Into the cemetery my feet take me,
a thousand years into the cemetery,
into the well of noise,
into the flesh,
into the stones that lie on the hearts and crush them,
into the black jugs,
from which the wine
of sausage-makers and gravediggers,
the wine of rustic gods wells up.

In My Mother's Garden

In my mother's garden
my rake gathers the stars
which fell down while I was gone.
The night is warm and my limbs
emit their green origins,
flowers and leaves,
the blackbird's call and the clatter of the loom.
In my mother's garden
I trample barefoot on the snakeheads,
which peer inside through the rusty gate
with flaming tongues.

From Now on I Will Go into the Forest

From now on I will go into the forest
and bury the cities and tame the night
with the knife of melancholy.
I will walk through the meadows on Corpus Christi
and press my cheeks into the grass
and stick my finger into the throat of the earth.
But my night will be like this: without fire and without salt,
I will kneel on the stones
of my deserted village
and search for my father—
I will listen by the udders of the cows and hear the pails
                                         whisper,
filling with milk.

I Know that in the Bushes Are the Souls

I know that in the bushes are the souls
of my forefathers,
that in the grain
is the pain of my father
and in the great black forest.
I know that their lives, which are erased
before our eyes,
have a refuge in the ears of wheat,
in the blue brow of June sky.
I know that the dead
are the trees and the wind,
the moss and the night
which lays its shadows
on the mound of my grave.

In Hora Mortis

'*La Luna, densa e gra[ve], densa e grave,*
come sta, la luna?'

'*The moon, dense and heavy, dense and*
heavy, how does it stay there [floating], the moon?'

Leonardo
Philosophical Diaries

I

The flower of my anger grows wild
and everyone sees its thorn
that pierces the sky
such that blood drips from my sun
it grows the flowers of my bitterness
from this grass
which washes my feet
my bread
O Lord
the vain flower
which is choked in the wheel of night
the flower of my wheat Lord
the flower of my soul
God despise me
I am sick from this flower
which blooms red in my brain
over my sorrow.

My eye torments me Lord
and torment makes my heart
into a blackbird
which does not sing
and my writing in the sky
strange grass
O Lord the star torments me
which floats through my sleep
with death and a pure soul's morning
Lord my eye sees what afflicts You
and brings my children to tears in your blood
O Lord my eye sees the house of the bricklayer
and the world's pain perfectly
and can do nothing to help
like the tree in the winter
which fells me in silence
my word my happiness my weeping.

I no longer know of a street that leads out
I no longer know of a street
come help
I no longer know
what will happen to me
during this night
I no more know what morning is
or evening
I am so alone
O Lord
and no one partakes of my suffering
no one stands by my bed
and relieves my torment
and sends me into the clouds
and to green rivers
which roll to the sea
Lord
my God
I am set out for the birds
to the exploding stroke of the hour
my soul sickens
and my flesh burns
O Lord in my word is darkness
the night that whips my fish

beneath the wind
and mountains of black pain
O Lord answer me
O hear me
I do not want this nausea alone
and to endure this world
help me
I am dead
and I roll like the apple
into the valley
and must smother
amid the forest of the winter
O my God I no longer know
where my path leads
I no longer know what is good and bad
in the fields
Lord my God in limbs
I am weak and poor
my word burns in sadness
for You.

Unrest is in the grass
the cottages are seized by unrest
I toll the bell Lord
my God
the doves are wild
the moon is restless too
and its sickle pierces my flesh
Lord unrest is even in the stall
and at the edge of the stream
which does not flee the snow
my God tree and fish too
are seized by the unrest.

II

Decay my God
who pounds my torment into dust
before the temples
Lord my God I am destroyed
covered already with weeds
and roots
O destroyed by stones
O destroyed in the fields
jealousy has destroyed me
in love
and spattered with blood
destroyed
I cannot dream
no one dreams
I cannot stand before you
I am destroyed in this time
which stabs me in the heart with its knife
O Lord who lets me kneel in ice and snow
for a prayer
and Heaven's distant mercy
Lord give bread and wine
and let me die now
and blow in the wind.

Your voice will be my voice
in bitterness
Your voice rattles this dying
in rigid furrows
which destroys me
O Lord my prayer stamps from night and fear
the sun
and the moon
Your voice is my voice
Lord I am in You
crushed by my torment
which sets my eyes afire
such that I burn my God in the flames
of Your wrath
which drives its thorn
of blood into my brain.

On the right sits the Devil
Lord who destroys my member
and clutters my brain
with stone and weeds and hardship
a long winter
Lord
in flesh that cries out to You
I will seek You in the dust
Lord so judge me
I have long been ready
my God destroy me
and don't let me alone
I cannot rest in my bed
I get no sleep
O Lord
annihilate me
do not leave me alone any more
not now
in this hour
not in the moon's fall
and not my God
before midnight.

I see Lord what I must see now
in the morning which does not want
this torment and not my bed
in which it snows
O Lord
who does not want my prayer
and devours my cries
behind the tired stars
rich fields
black farmhouses
who throws open my grave
who fells me with an axe
O Lord
who but loves man
the axe
and does not drink songs like blood
and death on green hills
higher
than the sea
O Lord
I want to see what must come now
my death Lord
and my passing away in tears.

When Lord my flesh turns
and this cold death in winter
night and hardship
stony and frostbitten
into flowers of pure wind
the disease
of my songs
these verses of disease
to drops of dew on green hills
Lord
when will my dying
free me to be nearer
to Your soul
which afflicts me so terribly?
When will my path
which gladly began in the snow
rise into the rain of frozen angels
Lord
my grave in the wind?

Why do I fear my getting old
my death which afflicts me
the scream?
I fear myself O Lord
I fear my soul
and the day which leans against the wall
and saws me into pieces
O Lord
I fear myself
I already fear the night
that is outside the villages
and behind the house
that bellows in the cows
and dances with the stars
O God
I fear myself
before You
and before the sorrow
which smites my mouth
I fear Lord
my grave
and my fate in darkness
O Lord death.

Death is clear in the stream
and wild in the moon
and clear
to me as the evening star which shivers
strange before my door
death is clear
as honey in August
this death is so clear
and true to me
when winter comes
O Lord
send me a death
such that I freeze
and language comes to me in the sea
and near the fire
Lord
death assails the base of the tree at night
and many a blackbird's sleep
in darkness.

III

Lord who lies no more
O Lord
who speaks my name
and blesses my songs of weakness
Lord
and the poppies of my eyes
the sorrow
O Lord
who informs me of when
I must die
and where
and how
and destroys with the angel's flight
O send Lord
the grain
how You have sown it
to the poor
who take shelter
outside cold barns
and freeze
Lord.

Wake up
wake up
and hear me
I am inside You my God
wake up
and listen to me
I am alone with You
long burnt to ashes
and dead in the stone
which strikes no fire for me
wake up
and hear me my God
I am already tired from the frost
and sad
for my day fades
and no longer comes any more
what was
O Lord
freezes me
my pain is without end
my death soon comes
for me.

Where are You Lord and where
is my happiness?
My solace is gone
and my dice
my God
the morning came and went
in hardship
where is what I am no more
and where the sleep
and the sweet smell of limbs
honey
leaves
and wind
from the Mount of Olives
Lord
my God
who describes the moon to me
at midnight.

Time is extinguished
O Lord
my word that came bitter
and dark
Lord
too dark for the earth
my torment is extinguished
my hunger is drained
and my heart in nights
that are tilled up
with the plough of songs
time is without end
yet filled with the need of dreams
which I do not want
on my stone of dying.

Tomorrow Lord I am by You
and far the world
which I do not need
and which doesn't sow my seed
and not my sorrow
which has deceived me
O Lord
my God
I want to be awake now
for my death
and for the rain
Lord
which now washes me
of fear
washes my spring
of this winter
Lord
sprinkle the poppies on me from jars
black
which have long turned to ashes.

IV

I want to pray upon the hot stone
and count the stars which swim
in my blood
Lord
my God
I want to be forgotten
I no longer want to fear the day
which comes tomorrow
I no longer want to fear the night
which I suffer through
Lord
my God
I no longer fear
what may still come
my hunger is already extinguished
and this black torment
is drunk up.

I want to praise You my God
in this solitude
and every fear scatters
and each death grants my eyes light
my God I praise You
for as long as Time exists
I am no longer alone
I am by You
and joyful
the birds are dispersing
black
and more
black
their number explodes
the moon screams out
but I am
gone.

Lord let me forget
my soul
and the eyes' torment
and the tired lips' dagger
and the green fires of far cottages
each pond's maw
forget
Lord
my God
this day
which splits my cry apart
which I cry
and many birds in passage
my anger is dismembered
and my blood gushes
free.

The birds oh the birds
the black night
my blood
O Lord
are cutting me up
all the birds
screeching the yellow
the tongue burns
cutting
oh in blood
the knives God
I drink my flesh
the knives
long dead is
my red
my green
my thorn stabs
cutting
oh
cutting
oh
cutting
oh
oh
oh
my
Oh.

Under the Iron of the Moon

The year is like a year a thousand years ago,
we carry the jar and strike the back of the cow,
we reap and know nothing of winter,
we drink cider and know nothing,
soon we will be forgotten
and these verses will fall like snow outside the house.

The year is like a year a thousand years ago,
we peer into the woods as though into the cowshed
of the world, we tell lies and weave baskets
for apples and pears, we sleep while
our muddy shoes rot outside
the front door.

The year is like a year a thousand years ago,
we know nothing,
we know nothing of this going down,
of sunken cities, of the river in which the horses
and people are drowning.

Not many die
for a house
in the desert
or for a withered tree.

Not many die
for ash
which was fire,
for the wine
of a deposed king
or to celebrate
a general
of scorched fields.

Not many die
for one another,
when seeds blow
and death and birds
blacken the clear skies
in the spring.

No,
not many.

They will wake up and be forgotten
in the laughter which rolls down from the hills,
in that storm of wolves,

which blasts their sheep's heads over the smoking cities
to dust
O don't turn to dust

in your hunger inexhaustible to the edge of the stars.
They will dance at night to the sickles of verse
and pierce their eyes

on immortality.
O do not turn to dust.
Pull your oars hard against your bones

and batter the wind
which mourns neither east nor west,
yet the torment which torments them is never destroyed.

The cock crows through a sheet
of flesh and gorges
itself in my blood
that saws apart
my chest.

He drinks my red
like a moon and laughs,
such that the stars
dance red
on the mountaintops.

In the mountains stars descend upon the pounding rain
when you touch the lips of my poverty
and below the church tower
in the wintry bridal bed
you predict the stroke of the exploding clock.

Mouths wallow in the river of wheat,
soundlessly the streams shimmer
in the voices of the moon's night
which rise from deserted ponds
into drained seas.

Scatter the salt of your eyes to the gulls,
but
open what you in never-smelt summers
smothered
and rot apart in the wound of my mouth.

Inside this wide-open sky of the mouth
many die and think of a day
which on green tables
and in cold dishes
of pink ham ended
with a sigh.

Yet their love is lost
like the wind winding
around the base of rotted trees
in the white of the north snow.

Their love is lost
in gloomy forests
which grow old in the sobbing of stray deer
from cloud to cloud.

He was already alone in the morning
with the birds under the sky
and said to himself that hell will be green

when the flowers sprout above the stakes.
He drank from the well of his mother
and shut his tired eyelids on stone streets

that are strange to our tongue all our lives.
In the summer he was sick
and saw the moving clouds rise

out of grim dreams,
a warrior with a burning throat,
he laid his hand lonely

on the lovers between the dead hills,
when October came
he was as strange as the snow

on the broken peaks of the mountains,
and his voice rang hollow
and parched in his milky grief.

No one bears this letter in his grave
which wintry
plays the rising moon for a fool

at the height of a well-besung life.

The white flowers of my spring
blossom in the blood,
only grief blows my dying through the deserts,
only the grass singing in the sky writes songs
where heavy clouds weep the grim March days,
we are no longer an ear in the river and no prayer in stone,
the rower of the stars dies,
the blue asses with empty jars pass serenely
through the brown leaves.
When will my God tell me where and when
time drives the thorn into my flesh?
The night burns the hours out for me,
The brickwork plunders my heart,
I want to blow away,
my frost depends on the leaves, sleep in strange houses,
the light in my prayer bores madly into the valley
out of exhaustion,
and a ghost raises the summer,
the dead in the grave
where my sore lips' diseased suns pull
over this green world with sleepers of red ashes
a blanket of moon and milk and wind and tears.

My despair comes at midnight
and regards me as though I were long dead,
the eyes black and the brow tired of flowers,
the bitter honey of my grief
drips down on this sick earth,
which so often keeps me up on red nights
to see autumn's restless dying.

My despair comes at midnight
from bewildering dreams of sun and rain,
I say so early, that I laud everything
and feel strange outside my door and my fear,
many thousands of years fall from the cold walls
and bring me a piece for the winter.

My despair comes at midnight,
the valley is different, the moon floats on the meadow,
the angry evening's broken sickle leans
on the windowsill and regards me.
I know well that I am as broken
as this sickle, no one deceives me now,
not even the river still rendering its decision
before morning.

Under the tree and under the river you are strange to me.
You, on the face of the unbearable sun,
black night, acquainted with the beast
in gashed forests,
my love at a lost
staggering towards the floating moon,
sick beneath the blackberry bushes,
over the roots laughing like
a snake hissing
under the blow of my stick,
thirsty on the hillsides,

O my mother's dream unto the marrow of the earth,
this loneliness in summer's singing chains,
hair of ash, your limbs
are withered and in the mortar
of my grief burnt forever,
until this memory sends her holy snow
into valleys gnashing together
and the frost makes songs and desires
freeze in the shivering air.

You, to whom I was faithful over a winter,
through the fire of the summer I heard
you calling—a flash of lying eyes,
I destroy myself in the corner of your heart.

The sleeper is in heaven and in hell
at home and hears organs
out of flowers and drinks a dust
from wintery limbs.

His solemn promises die in the forests,
on dry tree trunks
he reveals what was and goes
down freezing into the drunken valleys.

In empty houses his brain drives the thorn
into the fluid flesh of a forbidden love.
Unearthly he returns in the morning
and still holds the dream of the many dead in his hands.

Under the fire's breath
your arm resists
in the sunken valleys,
with early morning
the rising sun of your limbs adorns itself
and buries itself into lips deeper than the night.

The ash of the earth's sad hours
is no longer between us
outside the rusted doors
as a wind grown wild in dreams
opens your raw lids' silence
and becomes this heart's tree and torment
and honey drips from wintry roofs,
sweet snow from the brows of the world
for a moment of love cascading
from blood to blood
on these shores of foaming apple blossoms
inside these chains of the spring
which will leave me alone
with a bursting breast full of torment.

The rain of these days
only reaches the rusted heart of the night
in the black passages of the dead

who hang with bats under the rafters
and with grating fingers
angels in the darkness trace between the stars

which dance over the pigs and chase cows
in their restless sleep
with the lowing and whispering of the milk between white
limbs.

Often one stretches his forsaken leg out of bed
and lets chin and world dream
on the dusty planks of vice

where the moon trembles before the curtain
in the worn words of vulnerable sisters
who praise God in the sweet bread and in long speck strips

until the wine fills their brains with skies
made of ash and the grass
curls up their ruined feet

they swim upon yellow breasts
through the ephemeralness of sad springs
girls in black coats filled with the smell of apples

from their astonished mouths out of poverty
pour their maniacal wails
over my face of stone and tears.

Listen, fears blow
in the wind,
many children's eyes
shut tight
in restless streams.
Wilder cry
the birds
of my death,
listen,
fears blow
in the wind,
what I lost
comes shivering
back,
in death, many raise
white sails
with sore hands
holding
tired stars
and bewailed summers,
listen, my brother,
sister,
listen,
fears blow
in the wind.

Sleep beside me, be quiet, I must grieve,
I begin my journey once more, I count star
and plant in the moor and seeking your songs
I stir the dread in my pain
which gives my voice no limit
        and my mouth no word.

Keep to your fears and fall into dust,
cast an open eye up gloomy stairs,
I include you in my prayers just like my mother,
loving a white moon and naked ribs of cold forests.

O do not come during my going after sombre dreams.
Tell me, where was I yesterday? Was I not with you
as I lay content at the edge of the fountain
heaping up the dry earth of strange graves
and giving up to the cold wind
the sand of long obliterated tracks on my shoes?
Tell me?
        You do not understand me.
Sleep beside me, be quiet, I must grieve.

The dead have made ready the land
and given the fields peace and unrest
and the sun to the hills and to the forests darkness
which will haunt us tomorrow.
Our shelters are abandoned. A thousand springs drift
from the seas into my mother.

Morning after morning
talk to God
about the joys
and the fears of your children.
in the wheel of ephemeralness.

In the crater
the sins there
turn grey too,
what was,
death and fire
under the dust
of the locked door.
In long-forgotten seas
swim the stars
of your despair.
Noiselessly watches
the broken spring
of the dead
from the grass.

Above the fire
lick the flames
of jubilation,

under the roofs
of dusty farms
and gentle chapels.
From the coffins of night
climbs the angry moon,
pulling the death shroud of winter
over the pale shoulders
of sad meadows and sick streams.

The night dissolves at the gates of old walls,
the moon hangs restive, the earth seeks
to hold on to last summer's frost
and stars stand white on the mountains,
with green eyes dumbly staring
down from the trees' wearied lids.

I bring contempt into the valley and many say
that I bear only death, a dream and jealousy
in great baskets for this going down.
The stars curse! Strangely, the day falls
into its furrows near the river flowing
far below into these fantasies
with the stern words of my winter days.

The bright iron of the moon
will kill you and the unyielding
claw of a giant bird
in whom
you confided your grief
in the winter.

The forest will wrap its bones
in disquiet,
and the wind
throwing you down,
striking
from the white hiding place
of rotting deer.

The sun will bury
its holy wound
beyond the dying forest
and your lips of fire
will flame
into laughing flowers
of death.

Your grave
will be dug
in the south,
your death
will blow
in the south,
your face
is scratched by thistles,
your cup
is shattered by birds.

Your grave
will be dug
in the south,
your death
will blow
in the south.
Your valley
will forget you.
You come
no more.

Do not try to sing my praise
and laud my poverty
behind the wing beats of autumn.
Do not try, in my twisted joy
and my wheel-tortured voice,
to prod the fear from my fingers.
Do not try to console me,
for the winter belongs to me alone,
with footprints in the snow,
and the clatter of scattering hoofs,
and the clockwork in my chest
which knows nothing of dying cities.

Do not try to steal my count of hills and rivers
which are the summer's companions.
Do not try under the blade of my ploughshare
to break up the grass which sings my affliction
for some despair composed of ashes
and a rotting mouthful
made from the valley of these incomprehensible people
who lack a sea and lack a conscience.

It seems that I was much younger,
yet younger than those who already died,
I saw cities and the strain in my eyes
was the summer's moaning in the streams.

I was younger than the ones who often hurt me
and who have long forgotten my name
behind the loom, under the hammer,
or in the rough stroke of the harrow.

It seems that I was much younger,
and hanging among the clouds in the sky in March,
fairs setting up without funeral banquets

and hearts charred black,
and with April I was on a journey,
flying down rivers with birds,

laughing amid the bushes
and with the grass I was sad.
In the rooms I saw

many dying who loved me.
But I was chosen to speak
to the wind.

It seems that I was much younger,
I smelt wild requiem Masses,
wild stars,

churches standing in a sea of wheat,
the cheek of my hill
was always

acquainted with my anger.
I was just so tired
where apples drummed and the winter sang

from a thousand seashells.
The day passed sighing,
the year stood on the wall
blackly, disturbed by the fears of my time.

It seems that I was much younger.

Beyond the black forest
my thoughts strike their tents.
The broken rocking horse
of summer has stood
the moon in snow.
On a silver tail perches
the lost sun
peering down on the helpless villages
which have remained alone
with the cider of warriors
and with the soil of fear.

Only the serpent of fame protects you,
spitting its green among the rotting leaves
and retreats
under the cold torch of night.

The stone speaks of the sins
between the fire of the island
and the wreck of the night.

The rescued have a suit
of fame wrapped about their flesh
and the honey of the dead
put away in their double breast.

Beyond the grass and beyond the city
trembling from these thoughts,
the shy children sleep,
the black dogs dream
who soon haunt me in April.

The stone speaks of the sins
between the fire of the island
and the wreck of the night.

God hears my prayer too
with morning in the wheat field
where the wind
gathers the children of noon
and the sleepers on the wall
take a rest
from their brains.
God hears me
in the gloom of the rain
and on those paths
of bitter grass and bare stones
across the death's heads of night
which shatters in my dreams
out of fear.
God hears me
in every corner of the world.

The spring is your deathbed.
In the mouths of foaming bushes
you return.
From your children no tears are left for you
and from the men no shadows
                in your unruly hair.
The light drags your lies through the fields,
the tracks of wild despair
blacken your face
that is shown on a hideous cloud
of canvas.
Many forests fall to ash
amid the fire of your angry soul.

No tree and no sky
will console you,
nor the millwheel
after the cracking of pine logs,
no dying bird,
nor the owl, nor the scurrying partridge,

it is a long way back,

no bush will protect you any more
from the cold stars
and bloody branches,
no tree and no sky
will console you,
in the crowns of the shattered winter
your death grows
with stiff fingers
far from the grass and wilderness
in the expressions of fresh fallen snow.

Beyond the black forest
I burn this fire of my soul
in which flickers the breath of the cities
and the blackbirds of fear.
With bare hands I kill these flames
which climb the air into the brain
and quiver in my name.
My heart drifts like a cloud
over the rooftops
along the rivers,
until I, a late rain, return
deep into autumn.

The last day is trapped
in this beer glass and in despair,
it mounts with the birds behind the house
and plunges into the black pond.
No shout stops these hands,
these raw hands
and this protesting heart.

The shadows inscribe April and December
above the doorway
and discuss trees and diseased girls
and destroy the saying
in a pink slice of ham.

The last day is trapped
in this beer glass and in despair.

The wind blows imperceptibly
across the land.
Already the winter stands me up
in the high north
and hurls me into
its silent robe.

From late harvests the frost
Meets me again.
You don't get up.
You speak only in anger
The hunger of your limbs
flings me into autumn.

During sleep the night
hands out the great medals
of ephemeralness.
No dream moves me.
Outside the window at night
I hear death in the trees.

O this spring
which lies broken.
O this summer, dead,

on white pillows.
I have vanquished
the grim autumn in you
and flung open
the door to winter.
I fear the late nights,
long and clear.
Embittered I now search
in the park, what was.

Come under the tree, there the dead
rear up, the proud mouths of night,
and in dreams the white skeleton
stands the sleepy moon on the wall.

Spring flows down with the stream of limbs
into that fragility of wild birds
waiting on the banks for their desperate flights,
where the voices of the clouds gather
and the drowned children in the branches
       sleep in green wreathes.

The winds are getting old and the lips,
before the message from the valley comes to die
the sun and mouth part forever
and silent walks the time of summer on singing sticks

back into the morgue
from which the moon has risen with tired eyes
behind the black fingers of the forest.

Before winter assaults me
beyond the hostile farms
which blanket their music in snow and sweet smoke

—the children and dogs are asleep
under the stream's weariness,
the blackbird forgets you as well and the cup,
the smell of grim years in mute gardens
holds dialogues with tree and shadow—,

I want to put these shoes to sleep
and forget the troubles of the long war
and meet my brother at the cemetery
for evening's mourning between two gravestones,
one for Father and one for Mother,
and the blowing of the wheat over the mounds
admits my psalm of the earth
which will bury us with fear and scorn
beneath the dreaming limbs of the sun.

Let me see the crow's feet of the winter
and your eyes that changed
into strangled blackbirds
and that heart which you have exposed in the field
so that it hears the knives of the wings sing.

Let me see the evening fall apart before your face
which can never go back inside the house
wherein the he-goats of Christmas Eve laugh
amid the spurting of your embittered blood.

Let me hear the voice which finds no echo in the trees
and resounds around the farms in the valley
without the consolation of the forgotten rooster or the
                                destroyed mother.
The pond shows me where your anger rises
with red eyes and a cage for your songs
in this broken hand.

Now my death is near and close to the winter,
The valley dreams restless and keeps me awake
and some wind which writes on the frozen roofs
the names of the days and nights.

Once again in the sea of the wonderful wheat,
I am back tired from my strenuous flights
still listening to the talk of the old walls,
but far from the anger of the never-loved cities.

In old songs and shattered eyes,
where the moon timidly drives the dark harvests,
I want to see the dead's deep buried sun
on green hills in strange skies

and the early summer's dust in the evening wind.

Forget me in the rooms,
extinguish me before the gate,
let snow from white peaks drift
in my old age,
O forget me,

slowly will my death
in the cities of the south streak
the towers of happier days with wind,
O forget me,

I am long gone in March,
and with the words of the tree
which dies every day
beyond the mountains
snow-covered,
forget me,

tomorrow is only the smoke
of yesterday,
from a thousand mouths
of black rooftops,
death,
forget me.

O forget me
wintry in the valleys,
turned towards bleak hearts
and dreams
like the beating gulls' wings
of night.

November came everywhere
        everywhere
from freezing forests

a sad music before hollowed
        graves
conversing with each other

until the moon sinking late
        over the church tower,
tightened its veil.

November came everywhere
        everywhere
perhaps so that the snow will melt

on the cheek when the
        bells
shake through the frost

and through the blustery sea our
        mornings
regard the unmoving mussel shell of spring.

A flower,
a white flower
drank my anger
in this lonely city
and will know nothing more
of clouds and trees.

In its eyes wilt the children
of restless flesh
and sad songs
that are not sung any more.

Where shall I hang up this desperate hour,
this hour which extinguishes me
before the snow sticks to tongues
and the roses of the desert
amid the tattered white?

A flower,
a white flower
drank my anger
in this lonely city
and will know nothing more
of clouds and trees.

The apples roll in the grass,
in flowers the blood wallows
before long winters, tiredly
the funeral procession goes
uphill to the cemetery,
to the shoreless ones
who peer charred
from the laughing mouths
of the earth.

The sun darkens
over the white of the hills
in the autumn wind
which pierces through white fences.

Silently on the walls drift
the birds,
in the cords of the soul sings
the flesh.
Far below the millwheel makes
heart and brain tremble.

The earth
baptizes my children.
Shadows fall
from a withered night.
The blood of kings drips
in the valleys of warm bread.

The stars have
the speech of eyelids
which dream
of human eyes,
of hills
which are carved up
by the knives of toil.

A curse be
on this agony of winter
which drives the smoke
in homeless forests
through the milky stalls of the world
which chokes this faithless sleep
on the shores of pitiless dreams.

My children come,
when the sun falls apart with a sigh,
to see the oranges
which hang under the tile roof of my cottage,
and make their faces sound like bells.
Where the sadness grows on the wall
the blackbird in the stone sings to me,
which death sent from my fields,
sings
     and sings
in the kernel of the silent July night.

Between the rafters the gulls plunge
joyfully into the sea with wild hearts,
from the sweet fruit I hear the voice of the Orient
again
     in my fitful sleep
which castigates me with the deserted moon
and the sharp hiss of the snake.

The sea is a shadow of my DEATH,
the black ships rise up in the south
and PERISH on the shores of long winter nights.

Forgotten harbours shimmer on the coasts
of the East and my language flutters
downwards on white-enfolded islands
and higher than the stars in frost
and with the wind of no-longer-approaching oars.

Orange trees stand irretrievable.
The waves of early days are fleeting.
The snakes write in the sand of Mogador
DEADENING their limbs' long journey.

The grapes hang succulent in the black
forgotten gardens. Tiredly blows
the evening wind into this room. Strangely rises
the full moon
over the crooked ridge.

The rivers flow different.
The agony flowers irreal in the grey night.
The brother's life lifts the red eyelids
of ruined cities
with a shiver of memory.

The wind blows dying away over guitars
and broken hearts, the night blows
into red windows, dead games,
where dark times close in from the East.
Ominous are the steps of the faraway dead
and falling stars on the ancient hills
of the long-drowned city.

Tomorrow will be
what was
switched
with the sky
and the blood of the sun
dripping down
into the snow.
No prayer
will console me
in the evening
and no tree
will understand.

Into the mountains
my grief must fly
and the blackbird
must watch me
at the fresh grave.

Where does the wind
drive me,
my heart,
my brain,
down
into the city,
across
into the green
of washed-out hills,
      to
the moon
of strange women,
blurring together
white
and red
on the bare
churchyard wall,
in this forest
which blackly
stretches its legs
and laughs
in the pond,
flying up
wild

into the blow
of forgotten birds,
where to
my wind,
my heart,
my brain,
my tears?

Do not partake
of my hunger
which
fed me
in winter,
don't freeze
and forget the bush
which
fills my mouth
with leaves
and tears.

Wait at home
until I
am back
in April
and the voice
of my songs
drinks water
dead
in the stream.

Like the wind
    he runs down,
    like the wind
his knife hangs in the trees
    which cuts a heart
    out of a yellow sun
beyond the forest where his spring wife
    weaves bleeding dreams,
    digs only for him a grave
    and spreads a linen shroud out
    for his bloody feet,
digs for him, digs for him.

Like the wind
    he runs down,
    like the wind
drinking only fear and sorrow
    which wheel in dreams,
    a fiery autumn
    which coils death's pain
    in golden shadows,
dark words in a beach leaf
    on the wind,
    he runs down

like the wind,
brandishing a cane from the pure earth,
beating heaven
such that from the open wounds of white clouds
mornings drip to shiver
in his winter's singing.

In the fish
and in the birds
spring lies on a bier.

The moon speaks with the trees about the winter
of forgotten names
which rot in great baskets
with one face shrunken together.

From shimmering cups we all drink
the days of flowers
caught in grey and green
like drunken nightingales.

We drink and wear black clothes
in our own house
because

in the fish
and in the birds
spring lies on a bier.

My death soon comes
over the field, tiredly,
when the shadows
of black raves fall
in the grass
and the tree behind the house
shuts its eyelids
in the snow
and an approaching winter's
words drift . . .
      The sick soul darts
no longer overhead
looking about
the village.

When we shut the milky windows dying
      and make a fire,
      so that the voice of winter sings
in our flesh of the fallen summer
      and a good word crackles
      in the green stove,
the wound grows in a forest of tears,
      the black mirror of the water
      and the lamp of the war which is over,
we are afraid before the ice-cold wind
      and the biting snow
      which tears at our faces
      with red bird claws.

When we shut the milky windows dying,
      the spring becomes
      that which escaped us in March,
and above the country church tower the afternoon
      torments the birds and the grass
      and beats the dark drum
and lets paper clouds flap as this heavenly linen,
      the spring of broken doors,
      of angry priests and white flowers,
shooting through the forest with a thousand tongues

and freeing our names into infinite names
and plunging into our bleeding heart
which sobs in sleep and sorrow
of the early autumn's stony price
on lonely grave mounds.

The syllables in this rain-swept March
batter down the house of my fathers
and stir up the snow in folded hands
and press the eyes shut
of a madman beyond the church square.

The syllables in this rain-swept March
cheer up a lost sheep
and let the milk of dreams curdle
in seven villages facing mountains
which are made of ashes.

The syllables in this rain-swept March
fall apart across the water of the river
and come back during long nights
in sick brains and white tears,
sputtering over the green peaks
of a banished spring night.

My brain swims in the evening towards the sun,
my soul hangs in the broken branches,
my spring drifts in the forests, my summer,
I am tired again, oh, the cane of early days
is beating me with memory.

My brain swims in the evening towards the sun,
drinking the blood of night and the pond,
drinking the hills, valleys, dull words,
it cries in the darkness, cries before the timber
which creaks in rotten dreams of a crazed death.

My brain swims in the evening towards the sun,
my God, the twilight sleeps, the wind blows
upon barren fields, the clouds drive
restlessness into a death that buries me
and conjures black birds, my laughter's flowers
            in their insane beaks.

In the winter everything is simpler,
for you need no world,
nor the sea
and no one is going to kill you.
Comforted, you inhale the fury
of the beasts with the smell of the forests
which surround your peace and quiet.
Towards midnight snow mounts and ice
and under heavy limbs
your dead sleep.
You speak with them
as in that time of grain,
which they shear in darkness and lies
until the spring drinks them
under the sun
which steals its thorn from sick roses.

Our house separates the dead
from sun and moon
and lets grey flutes
to shatter along cold walls
and the eyelids of forlorn summers
freeze together under the copper roof.
With the blackbird groans
the river of green and red
and snow distilled from tears,
sleeping flowers
of midnight crow's feet,
a wind trampling
through the spider webs
and the laughter of a fattened pig.
Our house sets fire to poisonous clouds
and the forbidden cities of fear,
lies struck dead
under the rotten door
of my meagre winter's message.

How hard it is to find a word
for these ruined people
who cannot tell a dream apart
from the strong branches of the pear tree.

How hard it is to find a word
on this dusty street
which is as an enemy of my shoes
like the sun on the snow
and the water on the desert.

How hard it is to find a word
for my father and for my mother,
how hard it is to find a word
for all who watch me getting old
in an autumn stabbed to death.

How hard it is to find a word
in these days that are unmemorable.
How hard it is to find a word.

Speak grass, shout my words into the sky,
from peg to peg and over the roots
spring the wind's red and yellow brothers.

Hear how the brush burns and smoke pours
through wet mouths and cracks,
hear the cry of the dead in the poisonous weeds.
Poisoned are the clumps of flowers and laments.

My sick mother sits in the tree and weeps
and counts her tears like in Paradise,
and the forest stretches a thousand strings
from my breast to the face of the sun.

In the name of he who died on the grey stone,
I will send the birds south
where the wind blows through black forests
night after night and girl draws nothing
but sadness from the well,
I will sing in his name
and hear flowers in the blue skies of summer
looking down into valleys,
and open doors and mouths for forgetting.

A number of birds, an immeasurable number,
north of the sea,
my grave will be like his in the white of speaking,
in the folds of anger,
and in the dawn of captured seed
whixh turns to dust in his stiff hands

in the name of him who died on the grey stone.

The Insane   The Inmates

I am the prisoner, if I am not mistaken, for my clothes are prison clothes, and I have prison clothes on, do I not?

The brain is so unfree, and the system, into which my brain is born, so free, the system so free and my brain so unfree, such that system and brain collapse.

The hunchback with the water pail,
her with the braids all wild,
the nun tails white, the birds
black in a green image,

him with the forefinger
on his bloody forehead,
him with the yellow rope
climbing the cherry tree,

her with the black frock,
with the yellow pants,
him with the girl's face,
with the red rose,

her with the hazelnut stick,
him with the crying,
him with the goat bleat,
with the bandy legs,

In rags walks the man, in rotting shreds of cloth.
This the knacker wind says: I'm not stupid!
Siccing the legs of my trousers and the dog
which gets into my head and knocks me out.

I have on my conscience the crotch of a whore,
That which bites me on my back, this bundle.
I am disgusted by the shoes, the worn jacket's trim.
The soupspoon pokes in my trouser pocket.

There in the yard, there are the Pharisees,
a creature from the belt all the way down!
The truncheon swingers, squealers, marksmen, spies
in the bold boot-black of the prefecture.

The state is mighty, you're wilful and weak.
The uniform is the in-law of the law.
You keep your trap shut, keep your head in check,
walk through the forest which no one fells for us.

What ruins a truncheon on the head this way,
this I already know, one bellowing in my ears.
I am kitted out by an utter cretin,
driven insane by the sweat, tattered and shorn.

These trousers chafe and my backside is painting
The heads of misery on a thick wall.
Some get to drink while the others get to pay.
The thing you are, that which runs through your hand.

The reason of the dream dreads the reason of love, the reason of violence, the reason of death, for the sake of pure reason, which no one masters.

Starting with the effects upon the subordination to reason, we arrive at the inquiry for meaning, one that regresses, without leaving us in its wake.

her with the red hair,
her with the long tongue,
her with the turnip knife,
with the bad lungs,

her with the white veil
in the black door,
her with the long neck,
her with the cropped ear,

her with the rosary,
with the apples, the pears,
those with the yellow-white
vacant brows,

her with the fear of the doctor,
her with the cabbage-leaf hat,
her letting her blood drip
in the water of the pond,

I don't have a hold on myself, only planks.
Penetrated by their stare, I enter
my utter darkness, enter into these thoughts
where nothing else exists but stench and stone.

What is a prick? What is its perfect right?
What did it do now at three in the morning?
My voice box is dead, my stomach feels awful.
My brain has crawled back into my hind brain.

This is pestilence! This is irony!
And you, my moon, my yellow lord minister,
you piss on the world, on philosophy,
My last, great and most sacred master's degree!

My payday is wasted just like my whole life.
You are finished! You are long overdue!
To those things which you talk away, I need give nothing
                                              more now
Nothing more is left of my red brains but pulp.

'. . . if there is one less, only eight remain,'
this the brain says, this cracks in my little bones,
'those of the cranium, dashed to pieces
in the night,' which you hear now still gasping.

A clasped head, the maniac milk of my teats!
Officer, I am a man of such talent!
Up my ass, for there the world still has some heat,
when I go fetch my schnapps and my speck bread!

Clarity exists where the greatest helplessness pretends to be the greatest lack of clarity; in every composition, even in the composition of events inside the human (divine) brain.

Man, *who has the right to possess himself, who can possess everything and has the right to that as well; but no one has the right to possess himself.*

her walking through
the garden on tiptoes,
her with her eyes
mowing the meadow,

her with her hair
tied to the fence
wanting to scream,
her covered with scratches,

her coming from the chapel,
her looking from the window,
her with the rusty sickle
cutting off the flower tops,

her with the black stocking,
her on the hay wagon,
him, who those wearing red
skirts beat outside the barn,

You have no spade, no diamond, and no green ace.
The knaves of bells are trumping your fantasies.
The morning's red stinks like a great carcass.
The women are shrieking with their hysterics.

Blind from the mortar, in my wooden clog skates,
The smithereens of my skull shout the orders
From their prison guard's stupor . . . on the stair steps
the tripes of my soul are driving me crazy.

In the shadows my nonsense lies in ambush.
The temples hot from frost, the stick ready,
you scratch the blue balls of the dog annoyed.
And snarling he dictates his dictates to you.

Boozing has killed my Easter, my Pentecost,
the turtledove madness is tickling my leg.
The long nights have no influence in the least
during my diabetic insanity.

Torture, what am I worth by the bucket?
What, am I dead? What, do my threats of suicide lie?
My spume has turned half the world upside down.
I'm dying miserably in my prison garb.

My feet think and my brain goes far away.
From head to toe the world is nothing more than
a time of maliciousness, a time of depravity.
And the metropolis is murder!

There are irritating incidents which are a means to irritate, as, for example, the incidents between two incidents and incidents which make such irritating incidents known.

The line is penetrated by every line, which proves that there is no line and which proves, too, that one can consider everything as the line provided a character allows for it, what inevitably drives him into ruin.

her running from the kitchen
with the soup pot,
her with the mourning cap
on a red head,

her with the white
coat, with the blue
christening bow around the neck,
them looking in the apple basket,

them on the green milk
floating down in the dusk,
them in the black forest
going under in the cold night . . .

Schermberg 1949

Every star to me is a policeman.
The firmament is on the march, the oceans
a sea of truncheons, shit in uniforms!
The insanity is red on my prison's flag.

My loins are getting flogged as white as snow,
my red head swelled up in the noonday wind.
I go pummelled wherever I go wrong,
where I find nothing to eat any more.

In my eyes there twinkles the hurricane
of the ferocious and vicious laws.
I am my own dog and you are my companion,
who I hound into whoring in this jailhouse.

What kind of wine are you, my Herr Urine?
I walk past besotted through the shaven heads
of the under-underworld, through the ruin
and braid these pigtails for him from my hunger.

Garsten 1950

Ave Virgil

I sat upon the shore
Fishing, with the arid plain behind me
Shall I at least set my lands in order?

T. S. Eliot, *The Waste Land*

I
Wedding Party

Where did you hear myself in this cold . . .
    Where did I insert names and counter-names
into the narrative, into this oration
      out of poverty, my spectre . . . My word chose
sheep, swine, whipped oxen in calf,
      drank from behind the cow . . .
in thousand-year-old books
      my father's plough defaced the stars . . .

Octobers mowed down the truth,
      the wild wheat, the black cities,
to the very edges and into the darkness
      in a gull's cry, in an ass' bray . . .

I spoke for many, but to speak
      I had to fly up
like one of these birds,

flailing through the earth,
      converging with millennia,
boring through the firmament . . .

October, my companion, my humble father,
      the prodigious alcohol

scrawling 'hell, hell, hell, hell'
   on the walls of my guts,
beer drinker of the poor,
      frostbite carrier of mediocrities,

Me in the forest,
me in the cold,
me in the rivers,
me in the thick books,
me on the hill crests . . .
In the conversations of thrushes autumn confected its
                                                    triumph,
the serpent thicket gave a caning, made Raftery
rise up
'. . . and death will never come
near us, forever not in the sweet wood . . .'

I fought a single-minded winter
down in the valley,
I came up the autumn hillsides,
above me
the flocks of hopeless birds,
a killing of gill-less fish
below me . . .
               a paralytic priest
in the pulpit of the Milky Way . . .

Bride:
Nothing but dead faces
and behind them
nothing but dead trades

dead time and dead dying
dead pastures, dead fields
dead farms, dead cows
dead pigs, dead streams
and in the streams
dead fish
dead prayers, dead women
dead cities, dead winters
and behind them
dead science and dead plaints
dead autumn and dead spring
the dead madness of my dead soul . . .

Bridegroom:
What are the dead for without a sea,
what are the questions for, what are answers,
what are people for . . .

What are children for without spring,
what are conversations for without substance,
what are irresolvable things for, tell me
what are desperate dogs for . . .

What are snowflakes for which lack eyes,
what are traditions for,
what are words for, which do not comfort,
what is cold for . . .

What are mornings for without skies,
what are men for without women,
what are women for without men,

what are cows for without milk,
what are churches for without priests . . .

What are dreams for without the dead,
what are winters for without white,
what are graves for, what are . . .
what are screams for without weeping . . .

At three in the morning you wake up . . .
                                horse harnessing,
     Barrel rolling,
the wrecked piano gets swept out . . .

Pigs oinking . . .
sleep, sleep, sleep,
laughing, coughing, puking, laughing,
     a sentence you have already heard before
or read in a book . . . Closing of the cellar door,
     two horses, seven or eight people,
the voices from another shore . . .
     Zell . . . Caliban, the landlord . . . bursting laughter . . .
a tight space, shrieking, galloping . . .
     soon the sleigh is on the frozen lake,
     soon there is only a line on the lake,
     soon there is only a black stroke in the white night . . .

II
Winter Morning

Not that I am incapable
of pronouncing Your Name . . .

and they lynched me in the village square,
    tossed me in a dark pit
and spat upon my skull
    and yet fought over my prick,

Reverend Father,
    please accept my stammer,
give me a pronoun

which feeds none of my fatherly landlords
    with a cask,
no pig with its oink . . .

Legends, winters, overpopulations . . .
in sleep the wild leaves in the rainy autumn,
    that early stupidity of nights drunk up,
    black snow's relationship
to young couples . . .
    Wind and wind blowing and what is the truth
about the shadow of the world . . .
    the unmade bed,
the call of a sinister bird . . .

In the wheat field:

I did not pay the price for my life
before I distinguished the utter darkness from the utter
darkness . . .
did not praise the evening's shadowy fame too soon . . .

Ships, my brothers of the horizon,
    tell me about my mother . . .
 . . . where my brother stood on the shore,
    where my sister slept off her deceit,

I spoke of apple green and winter bran,
    I searched through my coat pockets . . .
I disseminated nonsensical psalms from the pulpit,
    quelled the bird cries in nothing but wheat . . .

Two thousand years after you,
    I discovered the cities,
I died on the hill,
    a charred skull from the north I . . .

The heat lightning of every star strikes me,
    which gave me the language of foreign peoples,
the alphabet of Virgil, the discourses of my farmers . . .

Two thousand years after you,
I am in the land, feeling sick,
freezing me in December's beds . . .

FREUMBICHLER INN

Through the window:

Who slept together with *my* chin,
    bore *my* leg in the war and *my* arm?
Not that I lived will I protest,
    not that I died and died *lower*,
not that I was *once* and *no one*
    remembered with a word...
        Not that I have not survived their jaws
and overwhelmed their feeble-mindedness,
not that I talked like a madman:

        smoked-pork apostles, depraved
          degenerate parishioners,
      choking you,

        those ushers in the forests,
      the doppelgängers,
        of impotent rivers ...

      in the confessional box
        the virus creeps between your balls,
      the sour psalm

      rained down on you
        with the fallen fruit
    of your children's children ...

and then:

What of this deadening is *Yours*
and what of this deadening is *my* share?
      I could not endure You without knowing,
You or me
or anyone sleeping with my name,
You, who confuses me with someone else,
who wakes me up for someone else,
You, who excluded me from their vanity,
You, who discovered me, You my only poetry . . .

In the village below:

Brewmaster, unworthy lord
      in archbishop's purple,
a shadow colonel in exile,

my voice is the voice
      of last rite's oil,
my voice is the voice of sorrow . . .

Priest with the watered-down wine,
      you are pawned
by a horde of parish clerks,

. . . the night is long before God,
immoral is the evening star . . .

you who pursued
      and whipped me
in the twilight state of the blackbird,

you who abandoned me,
    me, a head of cattle,
passed like beer piss . . .

No stanza have I bore for the amusement
    of this stupid province,
I sleep through my poetry unwashed.

           . . . and you knowing nothing
          of the rustle of the mountain ash,
          of other lives
          that were my life
          and were never my life,
          a life of many lives
          and unheard of
          and nothing
          and without question . . .

At the crossroads I read
    the small minds of farmers,
the lonely dying of the birds,
    in the streams I find
this cankered April,
    this ulcer,
the carcasses of winter deer . . .

On a foundation of prose,
    my poetry,
my betrayal,

here,
there.

Four times, five times, ever more urgent:

In these houses drinking my beer
in the conversations of air,
in the cold of thoughts
Not one of my grave diggers
unearthed
my early despair . . .

With this cheese-making odour, the wooden clog
clip-clopping

am I, for no reason,
the bone dust of my debt-ridden
neighbours . . .

Go away, go away wordless,
turn your back on their funerals . . .
that exhaustion with no sense,

the long evenings in the mill of rebuke . . .
go away, go away,
you need no judge . . .
go away . . .

Away

Where did I put my ship's ticket . . .
black man,
do you have my ticket . . .

who as I stand alone in the rain
in Piccadilly Circus

cannot say YES to the world

and cannot say NO either,
    and my ship's ticket . . .
where is my ship ticket . . .

ask the woman with the blue
    umbrella, with the blue heart,
with the blue compass point,

ask the man who folded up
    The Sunday Times
and where is he now . . .

ask in Trafalgar Square . . .
    O you in your parable
among nothing but strange men and women,

sufficiently dead and gone
    with the birds,
but where is my ship ticket . . .

on Lambeth Bridge and down below . . .
    and who cries down below . . .
and who remembers me . . .

and the skulls . . . the women
    with their lampblack necks,
these elegant doppelgängers,

nothing but philosophy
  and black walls and like a song
the tree, with black fingers

he departs into the night . . .
  the day before yesterday, yesterday . . .
Two lay in their own blood,

spurting it into the air,
  those puking on the upper deck,
their faces screwed up . . .

you must walk for an hour
  every day in Hyde Park,
down Oxford Street,

don't forget Charing Cross,
  the black girls
with the black hearts,

or that white heart
  inside their black skin,
who knows that . . .

III
Grief

Every day wakes up to some abuse,
 in my discourse is
embedded *the legend* of my sorrow,
 with a thousand year-old grief
I prevailed over my dirty life,
 but not over the rationality of the winter cold . . .

In taprooms you rip off
 the tattered shreds of your tragedy,
no forests, no merit, no archangel . . .

Above your poetry a swarm of birds mows,
 mows and mows a life imploring . . .
nothing for anyone
 in the proximity of this dream,
nothing for worldly lovers . . .

Fruit of rottenness,
 a wicked sun . . .
Temple ruins, broken pieces gathering
 on the rediscovered shore . . .
in gloomy courtyards books opening . . .
 Verses on abandoned walls . . .

       . . . *not* the perfect one,
not the dead man, who drove you into the cities . . .
         Trust in your song.

You plough the earth with your fragments,
cold begot you . . .
You, left behind by your creators . . .

First Song:

It is about the purgation of all our feelings
from the newspapers and from the streets,
from the concerts
and from the evening prayers,

it is about the purgation of our waking up,
it is about every good intention
and against all despair,
it is about the coexistence of twin absurdities . . .

it is not about this city and not about other cities,
it is not about this earth and not about another earth,
it is not about tomorrow and not the day after tomorrow,
it is not about all that is and what is not,
it is about nothing but the both of us . . .

Second Song:
Where in the world are you, if not
in these ears of wheat, in this degradation,
if not in my nearness, thus nowhere,

didn't you hear *why* I said NO,
didn't you hear my eulogy
which had nothing to do with pity,
only with our dead parents . . .

Where in the world are you, that I can
go and find you there. . .
But my death is as final as your death,
This I want to tell you . . .

Third Song:
Winter, ashamed of my speech I
called, called,
without an echo I was a withered tree
without roots . . .
           I asked the woods,
rotted with the rotting warriors
up to my temples, I lived no longer
a life even *close* to this life . . .

I did not mention the word of God,
           woke the toad and the partridge,
the fat pheasant and the hungry crows
with my wail . . .

Fourth Song:
Words seek words, migrating
from one mouth to another . . .
. . . and into your cities
and into your glooms

and into your silent word . . . nothing . . .
bearing grief, leading
other words' conversations
into open wordless books . . .

Fifth Song:
Lacking any talent I regarded the sea,
possessed by the idea of immortality,
by the soundless relapse into the ode of youth . . .
Wherever you weep
I am . . .
a thousand years
to this day
and a thousand years later
and always
with you
in your weeping,
and many
are dying for you
and many
for whom you weep
and always . . .
wherever you weep
I am . . .

Scenes in Verona

Frozen solid in my country, I have
    heralded the truth,
patrons, my facilitators,
    twice through the winter of poetry
in the uncertainty of the Milky Way . . .

I

    In the century of cows,
Catullus, 'gens Valeria . . .'
    In the parched valley
you led this dialogue with the dead,
    on black names you have
established your silence:
    Two bird shadows
    Two nevers
    Two without end

II

Enormous sufferings did not make them strong,
they invoked the future
and confronted you . . .
    Two thousand years too little lived,
this destroyed you . . . once they
were without time, were
without end . . .
    He wept, withdrawing into her dream,

awaited the superfluous wordings
  for her beauty . . .
she felt nothing,
  he entered this NOTHING . . .

  III

By what
  right to these places,
by *what* right . . .?

  IV

Whispering shapes drew the blacknesses
  over you,
broken chains, where you were
  scourging yourself with a scourge of birds, . . .
a monument to boredom on the hills of frost,
  the days stay black
and you in your hunger.

  V

At the foot of the grave I heard
  your voice
in the rising of the crows,
  with cheap lies I tried to hold you
on the banks of the river . . .

  VI

  Who wrote before me,
so that none lived before you

and none died
and none were in me,

who wrote before me,
so that spring was winter
and winter spring,

who wrote before me:
our names were *this*:
a *black* green,
a *dull* red,

who wrote before me
as the cold wind came inside
the cold graves and the cold dead?

VII

you in your shadows,
you in your waking up,
you in your time,
you in your fame,
you in your word,
you!

VIII

On the ridges of the Adige,
I learnt days and nights.

IX

With my finely honed knife
　　I scratched your beauty
into the rind of heaven,

I dressed your wound with snow,
　　and dried your blood like the wind . . .

X

　　For a long time I did not know
who they were,
　　I trusted their cries for help,
related to them the lament
　　of our lament,
for *my* land betrayed me.

XI

　　From the paintings I ripped the noble faces
of ancient families.

XII

　　The orders of night
endure.
　　you turn in in books,
the earth reins *me* in
　　with its thoughts.

IV
Your Death Is Not My Death

I

. . . seeing the way the mole tunnels . . .

II

Hymn to Mercury, hymn to Aldebaran,

III

before the rose the thorn,
    before the light the shadow,
before the old death . . .

IV

    the dusty chronicles,
the eight-hundred-year-old names
    have betrayed you . . .

V

Then I appeared before you and in your suffering
    as though you were filth
and could suffer me . . .

VI

that ludicrous phrase of your death
    never fails for me on the holidays . . .

VII

with a tally of despicable cows,
    am I the shadow of their amusement . . .

VIII

My shoe proves the sadness of the songs
    and few sing along with me, today no one,
        I no longer know *why* they are all silent . . .

IX

Leader of my prayer, I crush you
    out my useless eyes,
with a free tongue I speak to day labourers,
    in your name
I bandage the inner turmoil
    with sleep . . . with the treetops . . .

X

Until I came down, my knees hurt,
I trembled at the thought of my grave,
my grave, far greater than the grave of the longest buried
and yet higher than the one I lived
and died alone in another's grave.

XI

Death descended into this life in the end,
many were slayed while waking up,
going to work, exhausted, impassive.

V
October

On the pile of rubble the wailing of the mother
     means nothing,
the intercession of the drunken father nothing,
     the death report of the lieutenant nothing,
the revolt of the cardinals nothing,
     the accusation of the future nothing,
the weeping of entire peoples nothing,
the killing air nothing,
     the end of the oceans . . .

I dig up the buried beetles,
     the humiliation,
I raise my decrepitude

to my rotten mouth,
     to my shrivelled brain
in my morning misery . . .

In the night
     you calculate the firestorms of the world
with my fraternally feeble mind . . .

CHORALE
What does the day want of me,
asking me questions, a hundred thousand questions,

presenting names to me,
stirring up my mindlessness with its weeping . . .

What does the day want from me,
nailing me to thick trees,
wiping its blood into the corners of my eyes,
such that I see no land any more for the blood, nothing . .
.

What does the day want from me,
pounding stakes into my flesh and making me sing . . .

Song of the Butcher's Boy

You deftly cut the white
    body in two,
you misuse the tools
    of my weeping,
with both knives you stab
    October's skull . . .
my death, my dispatched bird,
    which convinced me . . .

I am, Father,
    preacher to the deformed,
above
    and below,
mightily herding
    the lambs in my head
together,
    I, the butcher's boy,
sitting with my PASCAL in the slaughterhouse . . .

on the doorpost hangs my brains;
　　for as long as I can remember
they rot . . .

When my morning, the morning of the world commingle,
when the sea emerges from the forest

and the houses take on the colour of the afternoon,
　　the pestilent face of the insipid summer,
when ninety thousand awake and a hundred thousand,

I pose to the ninety thousand
　　the hundred-thousandfold question concerning the lies
　　　　　　　　　　　　　　　　　　　of this world.

Dried up

Rome ruined
my awe
with the nausea
of its antiquity,

Catania, a bitch
at the foot of Etna,
Syracuse, a monument
to boredom . . .

　　　　　　In Sapri I slept through
　　　　　　that ugly sea
　　　　　　on a funeral stage . . .
　　　　　　bitten by pines . . .

the rotten strand
on the west coast
drew my tears
from the pores of the bathers,

I summoned waves
over them,
I murdered them,
vipers from the north,

their appearance
on the sand
made the tragedy
all the more laughable . . .

Reggio, Calabria,
dull blows,
clockwork . . . the deadly
knife sharpening of the trains . . .

that woman from England
pursued me
into the cactuses . . .
my heart broke hers . . .

Taormina, tropical February.
From Calabria
I promulgated
deadly letters.

VI
Who in This City

Who is the morning in this city,
by what right
other men more receptive,
not the experience of warriors,
not my fiction . . .

Who lived off me in this city,
made but an echo,
incapable of one line of truth,
provoked nothing but the sobbing of this dog soul
in the noon heat . . .

Who can't bear the blows in this city,
the fourteen-hour-long tribunal,
the unceasing interrogations of night . . .
Who wouldn't die in this city
at the edges of great sentences,
outside great books
going down, like the pigs
going down into oblivion . . . ?

You on the avenue of ideas . . .
                    mindless fields steam
in perfection.

Conquerors of the world:
                    Dante, Virgil, Pascal

KARAKORUM / MÖNCHSBERG

Where is your treaty with the fatherland,
that dirty piece of paper?

When you ask, no one knows where you are,
no one has ever seen you, nor heard,
the tree does not know your name, the city does not,
in no street have they sought you out . . .

When you ask, will the winter answer,
it knows nothing, the mayor nothing,
the governor in the Residenz nothing,
not even among the dogs are you the topic of
                                        conversation . . .

When you ask, they shake their heads . . .
When you ask, all are dead, deceased
for nothing and for this alone, who no one knew . . .
                    no one weeps for him,
as he was no more or no less like us all . . .

Decades sacrificed
        for some rainy procession,
for some ridiculous sermon for the poor,
for the constitution of a butcher,

for the cankered laurel
of uncouth fantasies . . .

Decades sacrificed . . .
    embroiled in conversations
of infinite Novembers,

I gave order to the disorder,
    I buried the rotting limbs
in the shadows of tall trees . . .

VII
With Me and My Land

Where I lived is
    to hear your obscene voice,
not a single verdict's sentence
    trumped me up in your shadow . . .

My relationship to the rivers
    stands between you and me,
I have but one idea:
    to squander this stupid land,
the hopeless streams with all
    the children and children's children . . .

I have my science
    from the potato diggers,
from the gloom of pigsties
    I have studied heaven and earth,
in the detritus of October apples I am
    my unceasing psalm . . .

Without you to see, I listen
    to what you say, I am always
in your houses,
    in the blackness of *your* house
I know *my* father

as the maker of my death,
as the bringer of my sorrow,
as the prime author,
as the father of my crimes . . .

Who speaks from the bush?
. . . the evening keeps silent.
They found me confused . . .
I knew no stanza, no verse,
but everybody rose up against everything . . .
as though I did not exist in their cities:
like a cold wind, like a curse of the elements . . .

With this sad land alone
don't think . . .
neither open windows, nor open doors,
just legible inscriptions on the gravestones.

(1959–1960)

NOTE

Ave Virgil originated in England during 1959 and 60, from everything in Oxford, and in Sicily, from everything in Taormina. For twenty years I had forgotten about it. Then I rediscovered it among other poems from that period, of which about thirty could be destroyed, and the reason to publish it now is the state of mind in which I found myself at the end of the 50s—the beginning of the 60s—recreated and concentrated into this poem as in no other. During this time, after graduating from the Mozarteum, my theatre studies occupied me as did everything written by Eliot (*The Waste Land*), Pound, Eluard and César Vallejo as well, and the Spaniards Rafael Alberti and Jorge Guillén.

Th. B. 1981

Later Poems
(1959–1963)

Vienna 1959

Where was I
in that time
which was my time?

I know nothing
of ageing
as it taints our begetters,
rolls out their faces.

Everywhere chains rattle—
Am I a dog?

My question
is unanswered
I hear the adversary
on the wind.

In October I go away,
I ignore
my village of a million,

but always there,
even under the palms,
is the word WINTER

I have come
to set the clock,
page upon page
are my attempts at this.

My hand is incapable
of the end.

I am still
among the tradesmen
who sat at their desks
with me in school.

I am shackled
to this uncertainty
on the winter feet
of my unrest.

Italy 1960

The New Rome ruined
my sublime awe
with the nausea
of its antiquity.

Catania, a bitch
at the foot of Etna,
Syracuse, a memorial
to boredom.

In Sapri I crossed
a calm sea
on a funeral stage.
The pine trees bite.

The rotten beach
on the east coast
drew my tears
from the pores of the bathers.

I summoned waves
over them,
I murdered them,
vipers from the north.

Their appearance
on the sand
made the tragedy
laughable.

I looked up
and saw
stairways of oranges
leading downwards.

Pesaro, dull blows
on my tired brain,
a deadly clockwork,
the knife sharpening of trains.

The lady from England
followed me
into the cactus;

my heart
broke hers.

Taormina, tropical February.
From Calabria
deadly letters
promulgate themselves.

I Am Famous in These Famed Fields

I am famous in these famed fields,
    I summon my summer, the dark days
of the motherly world,
    the pigs, cows, horses, the deer betrayed
in the isolated forests . . . .
    I am famous in these famed fields
and in the cold . . . I people the summer mornings

in knitting and furs, in strong belts
    I deal with hell,
I drink my milk for myself,
    I talk for myself with my words,
my foretold birth,
    my state of things,
my mistreated husband and wife . . . !
    From incense I descend banished
into the rotten forests of history.

I am famous in these famed fields . . .
    A chorale of every bell,
the neighing of the stars will make me clear,
    in every place I am in the highest balcony
for every one of my songs of a weary people,
    for them and for my certifiably insane earth . . .

I am famous in these famed fields,
    these temples without sleep . . .
the canine saviour of the morning
    will prophesize me,
the wind,
    the litter,
the frost, the banished winter . . .

Psalm

Cast my shadow over me,
     pay for my crimes
as You pay for my imperfection,
     for the irredeemable future of my nation,
change the time as You would change me,
     still my future with fear
and inscribe me in the hopelessness of the spring.

Do not have pity for me
     like my rotten dog,
deceive me, lead me into temptation,
     hasten the time which blows over,
the threefold wind, the blasted blackbird,
     the speech of my father
the speech of my mother.

Cast out of the morass I pray
     for frailty,
I implore filthy music,
     the morning's sharp look on the hillside,
I flog myself in groups and alone,
     swirling like the wing I come
a shameless liar who incinerates me to a whisper.

Trump up a charge which convinces them of my
        repentance. This experience from the war,
which undermines my self-assurance,
        the proceeds for the begging song
on the thirty-first of December.
        Trump up a charge which gloriously
overpopulates the abandoned cities.

The day after tomorrow my father's law
        shall blast open the doors,
trump up a charge on the water,
        at the top of the world,
a subdued complaint at the start of utter darkness.

You will not be able to drink all the purity
        in my prayer,
trump up a charge,
        which will be just to their faces.
        those faces surprised
at the abyss of faces,
        trump up a charge over me
and trample us into the winter.

Bible Scenes

For Georges Rouault

I left the mountains
When I turned around
No one asked for my opinion
Of the mountains

I left the cities
When I turned around
No one asked for my opinion
Of the cities

I left them all
When I turned around
No one asked for my opinion
of them all

I

Obscene birds
Astonish the snow
The east wind sharpens the dome

I would talk the years
Down off the walls
If I were not too low
For this priceless business

The madness of the stones passes
The soundless fall of snowflakes
Traces of vanities
I speak for many

But in order to speak
I must fly up in their language
Like one of their birds

II

The one-sided peace grows
out of the steeples
The lower courts advise

III

A drummer shatters the window
Grand pianos squeeze their entrails
In this rotten white

IV

Birds gather
Birds birds birds
They drill through the firmament
They guarantee the afterhours

V

In the sleigh
Weeps the suicide
He kneels to the darkness

He tries
He answered the questions
He kills the fingers of snowflakes with his blood

VI

When was October?
She sent him children
Dispatched them into his heart
She persuaded him

VII

He was a terrible father she says
He murdered everyone
The unstoppable alcohol is incomprehensible to him
The waste inscribes its name on the walls of his intestines
The snow shackles him to his country

VIII

He cannot go inside the houses
It makes no sense to beg
Everyone begs
Christ is their merciful precursor
The companion of their nails

IX

He is familiar with the forest
No one called for him
When they were calling everyone
He is against children with children
Fear him

X

From the paper flowers she peers
Into the white
She sucks in the rose of the cold
Her feet clatter
Under her flared skirts

XI

The heralds of the forest
Appear in her face
They fall apart
When she looks inside

XII

A lunatic
Goes about the yard
A girl with long pigtails
A waterhead in the archway
Snow chases them
The seventeen-year-old
Is killed between gothic doors

XIII

The dead chickens huddle
Against the wall
Their red breasts in this shroud

XIV

Schoolchildren stand
Around the pig

They beat it
On the back of its head
One tears off
Its left ear
The butcher deftly cuts
The white body apart
Above their wool caps the organ drones

XV

The lambs in my brain
Flock together
The blood is restless
In the slaughterhouse the butcher's son sits
On the pig trough
And looks
As though he were creeping into bed

XVI

On the door jamb
Hang my brains
For as long as I can remember
They rot

XVII

At the cemetery wall
I seek
The departed
With my hazelnut stick I beat
On the heads of the graves
I discuss with one of the corpses
The evening which is my brother

XVIII

Death a bird sent
Which convinces me
Tangled together
The branches shake in betrayal

XIX

How he falls upon me
And pushes my face so long into the snow
Until I pass out

XX

I am afraid of this loathing
I see after many years
That the wingbeats
Are getting stronger
As we have used them
Like children

XXI

The thirteenth village
The mouth of the jail opens
So what am I to do
With my answers?

XXII

In his wooden bed
I make
A day of prayer and penance
I am betrayed

In the dull vileness
Of my countrymen

XXIII

I shout
Famous testimonials

XXIV

Messengers
A cemetery green
Waitresses
The frost shatters
The colour of the evening

XXV

Without them I
Cannot come out
Beyond the forest
The third prayer procession
Awaits me
But I fail
To draw its attention

XXVI

I suffered more than the pastor
More than the teacher
And the carpenter
I suffered in the evenings especially
And in the night
I awaited the morning
With an axe

XXVII

I attempt
To change myself
With any death

XXVIII

This loner offends me
He is walking
Into mediocrity
However much I tell him
Given his intentions
He won't back down
He puts his foot
In the door

XXIX

The sales agents are here
We rejected them
At the crossroads
They made offers
Like swarms of birds
On our behalf
This bloody forest lane
Betrayed me

XXX

Suddenly snow fell
The windows shed
Their rules

XXXI

After they left
The taproom
He made him stand still
He beat him with his fist
And robbed him

XXXII

At this very moment
They were the same age
Buried first
The ceaseless falling of the snow

XXXIII

I am alone with myself
The door closed
The shadow of my interlocutor
Has been sent away

XXXIV

The snow is deep
You will be buried by it
Where is the messenger
I have listened for his footsteps
For an hour already
But the intruder is never
outside

XXXV

In his coat
He had a club
Which he used to kill calves
At the market
But early on
He saw
That the chaplain
Was a wretched fellow
Not even this aversion
Could free him
For a neglected murder

XXXVI

The snowfall stopped
Up his mouth
His curses
Are choking already
Deep below

XXXVII

He pulls
Up a spruce root
He presses it
On his neck
But this method
Does not hit the mark
He tries it
In his sleep
But he wakes
In the same condition

XXXVIII

They wash the corpse
Stick pine sticks
Between its fingers
They oil the white body
The chaplain sits
To the left of it

XXXIX

The birds perch
On the rooftops
All night the clerks have
With their absence
Prepared for death

XXXX

The butcher's helper looks
In the trough
He dries
His hands
The evening pains him
With the body of the not-yet-eviscerated pig
He spreads his apron over the trough
The altar of his father
He grips
His finely honed knife
He carves his name
Into the frozen fat
Outside the slaughterhouse door
The snow covers
The wound

XXXXI

The card player is
In the back room
Laid out on the icebox
The doctor puts
No more faith in him

XXXXII

The innkeeper is silent
The deer back away

XXXXIII

From his mouth
Runs blood
As though he had slit himself
With the white bone

XXXXIV

The sacristan studies the book
The rain does its work
The spring comes
And it gives the lie

XXXXV

The irregularity of the star
Reveals its bones

XXXXVI

The groceress
Runs into the darkness
She rows through
The oceans of shadows
She pulls off
Her apron
She stops
At the groans of the horses
She approaches this noise
On a thick rope
She will be sucked
Into the forest
She breaks her neck
In April the assistant forester stumbles
Over her

XXXXVII

With his knee the innkeeper props
The moon
He bites into a block of cheese
He fires up the tile stove
His son the warrior
He sits by the stove's door

XXXXVIII

The teacher watches the snowfall
With a torn jacket
When he walks across the square

He has still never
Lain with a woman in bed

XXXXIX

The pastor is left alone
with his breviary
Inconspicuously he stands at the window
And observes the people
In their black coats they remind him
Of death
The snow wipes him from the chalkboard
Of winter

Slaughtering Day Night

Pork colossi, piled ceremoniously on the cellar table,
in foul passageways of barrels, calves split open, tails,
the farmer went about with a red stockman's apron and a
shiny knife.
The night stares black at him with his murderer's eyes.
The moon dangles in his work, the black silent one.

All Hallows

The black pig, death's white helper,
with a red incision slicing open the lament, Mother,
and you with your sleep and I with my red,
and before the moon no word of the dark night . . .

I repress my scream and I fall, white snow,
I do not mourn, the sun's gaze has crushed me, Mother,
and on the white bed of pain I kneel black
and still have the answer's sorrow in my mouth.

At the Thurn Pass

Before white summits the shadows
of heavenly sorrow
sinking down into the dying valleys
of nights falling apart
where black on the shores the hills
the multitudes of birds mourning
deadly angels rustling

In the quiet rooms of death
restlessness
when and the breezes silence
the sickly farewell of the cheated
the days
that buttress supporting wind and words
seas and peoples

Shadows through an eternal distance
of laws
enormous fallen suns
one man's How and time
dies of thirst below
and never where the mountains' flames
border on the winter
the devastated cities

Walls of questions,
the wasteland of a merciless heaven,
when nothing from any of us through its glory
redeemed and the deceased
dream in everything
from the towers the shadows
penetrate everyone
when Never that icy silence
kills us and the others
a fallen word through us
ends the earth and what covers it
with showers with humiliation

Silence the evening leans
towards tomorrow and with morning the sun
looks down upon us that deception
its nature
the betrayal not unlike ourselves
in tattered words
the dead gape

In the old ice
the peaceful face
of the fictitious person
peering down where over the water
the terrified stars are
and the verdict like those figures
on the ground speak their language
those first-timers
who came from the top
wonderfully ending in that fire's
peace on earth.

Magic

Eagle-like
in an endless grave
twined with shadows
that kill the mind
the frozen air
where language ends
on the hillsides
the court is clearly in session

Ophelia in the Pond

In her white sleep her green eyes are awash
in black water, where the clearing is silent
and from the decay of her stiffened limbs
the sweet mist of her pain is ascending.

Her red stockings in the face of the moon,
her blue hands there below on the bottom,
the open eyelids, the putrefaction
Takes away the joyful smile on her lips.

In the Bible

In the Bible, a great tree stands for the dead,
in the Bible, the wind comes with cities in the night,
in the Bible, you will be reckoned by your evil deeds,
in the Bible, hell is about heaven,
in the Bible, you are blacker than the black night,
in the Bible, your mother and father talk and weep, each one
                                    in another language.

(1961)

I Feel the Moon's Too Good

Hamlet: That skull had a tongue in it and could
    sing once . . .

I feel the moon's too good
for greeting the Herr Gendarme,
I feel my hat's too tight,
I feel night sits at my feet.

I feel my brain's too dull,
I feel my head is unhinged,
I feel me my Herr Gendarme,
my heart is cut out whole too.

(1961)

No One Knows You (I)

'My feast of joy is but a dish of pain'
Chidiock Tichborne

No one knows you
and when you die
they slip on their coats
and bury you quickly.

Never forget that!

No one needs you
and when you die
they bang on the drum
and hold their tongue.

Never forget that!

No one likes you
and when you die
they trample your homesickness
back into the earth.

Never forget that!

No one kills you,
but when you die,
they spit in your beer mug
and you must pay.

(1961)

Skull Cider

Behind the stick fence
    beets already rot black,
the mortar trickles
    before the knees of women,
the summer springs frayed
    from the beans,
the well pole screeches
    a lumpen melody.

In the moon's horns
    the firs stand petrified,
the stablehand soaks
    his dull brain in beer;
in the fireplace
    shriek the copper pots
of the fat landlady
    at the undermaid.

The butcher pulls
    the knife from the belly
and flings it
    in the calf trough,
the tailor sits

on his old stool
and hears in the dark
　　his broken leg.

The cobbler kisses
　　his apple in the window,
the priest
　　creeps from his confessional,
the farmer spits
　　in the beggar's cup,
under the down blanket
　　the baker goes berserk.

The wild sow fears
　　my hazel stick
and limps silvery
　　in the starry night.
My sick heart
　　I must hide from her
so that today
　　there is no nonsense . . .

Beyond the forest
　　a taproom awaits me,
a stupid woman,
　　a mug of skull cider
where I can plunge
　　my loneliness
when my bones are already
　　stiff from frost.

The black speck
      cast a spell on my conscience
beneath the arm
      of the wooden Mary;
they envy me the last
      sour bites
and the maidservant too
      to whom I submit.

The hill dreams,
      the stubble fields sweat,
the moon extends
      its white tail,
the pigeons spin
      and the eyes flash
in their midnight
      dance.

(1961)

Almighty Tabernacle of Wind

Almighty tabernacle of wind,
Writing not to be read and not to perish,
Writing about grass and write about deathbeds,
Writing about me and write about you,
Writing of my inscrutable cold,
Almighty tabernacle of wind.

(1961)

To W. H. (I)

Three thousand years after the father
    I died upon the hill, the wind,

a charred skull, me, the north,
    the alphabet of Virgil, the discourses of great farmers,

three thousand years after the father
    I went through my land, feeling sick,

me freezing in September's beds.

(1961)

Horse Traders, Farmers, Grenadiers (I)

Horse traders, farmers, grenadiers,
a senior officer, a cardinal . . . and annual figures greater than
                                        the earth
of the old dead who walk through dark passageways,
vaults, who speak nothing, who only admonish you
and no writing and all great writings,
which are their books . . . now the villages avenge them
and ask, what are you and where and when . . . and know
nothing . . .
          that which is not,
which can no longer exist as well,
which the frost says, which the forests say behind you,

rotten, wasted, in withered branches
the wind pulls apart, the rafters groan

and what you say, which does not concern you at all,
and what you mean, no one is willing to understand any more,
and what you drink, which no one is willing to buy you . . .

Horse traders, farmers, grenadiers,
a senior officer, a cardinal . . . the words,
which are nothing to one who is nothing . . .

the doors black,
you still know no names,
     the cockle stoves do not burn for you,
the beds too,
and your father's dog, which will tear you apart ...

(1961)

Guard Me

Guard me from east and west, men,
drunken traffic directors of my roofless belly,
prosecutors of the frost, petitioners of February storms,

warm and spotted the cow, the footcloths warm,
the milk warm and the sky, the lice-ridden bed
and the woman who won't say no and won't say yes to me.

Guard me from east and west, men,
my sled-runner king, my bowel butcher
with the subpoena before the court of the winter cold,

I want to perish and ascend into hell,
to leave out my life, the bottommost station,
which is no song, no prayer, no weeping, no nothing!

(1961)

Cankered April

Keep going, keep going without a word,
    turn your back on their funerals,

Priest, with your watered-down wine,
    a horde of parish clerks have you pawned,

Brewmaster, a shadow colonel in exile,
    drunken archbishopric purple,

the night is long, the Evening Star is indecent,
    my holy breath is driven away . . .

Keep going, keep going without a word,
    turn your back on their funerals,

on the foundations of prose, my poem,
    my betrayal in this cankered April,

in the ulcers of the winter deer,
    between the dying of the black birds,

in the wild outcry of the river,
    in the death chambers of fame . . .

        keep going, keep going without a word . . .

(1961)

Weeping over Inconsolable Days (a cycle of five poems, 1962)

In the Valley

In the valley with his mouth silenced full of silver
about the bones, about those he stumbled on,
who went to the mayor and reported: a man,
no man, a grenadier, a white-faced skeleton
with a helmet on his head,
      on his bleached skull,
a grenadier, you know, you know nothing . . . 'fetch
it here, bring it to his mother . . .'
N.W., 1945 with your horse,
that one was a steed, too stupid, that I don't know,
was it still March, was it already April . . . the wheat was
not good, I didn't know what to do, for such a man
after fifty years can often
          still make our women weep . . .
          I kick him, I let him lie, I reaped
my autumn here and will he
      ever be compensated for the east torn off?

Warrior

The saddle and equipage rotted where he fell,
the sun rose and knew nothing of him,
he spat upon it, but it pushed him down
and with its brow pressed his hair
and his full belly deep into the spring soil.

The birds shrieked and no longer stayed
each year as well, along the wall
they flew and through the green garden,
they pecked at the apples, the ripened pears,
the saddle and equipage left lying at their feet.

No king succeeded the royal highnesses
who knew to sing nothing of his caprices
when he was twenty-four years full of pigs
and cows, morons, water-headed children,
stupid brothers of Jesus, last will louts with no future.

A Stanza for Padraic Colum

Across the Door . . .

At three in the morning you wake up,
    harnessing horses, rolling barrels,
the oinking of pigs waxes over your sleep,
    again laughing, coughing, vomiting, laughing,
the moon climbs through the window, snorting horses,
    slamming of the cellar door, seven or eight people
from another shore,
    Zell, Caliban, the innkeeper, a burst of laughter, shouting,
galloping . . .
    Soon the sled is on the frozen lake,
soon but a line is on the lake,
    soon but a white line is on the lake . . .

Birthday Ode

In the pigsties
you, with your dog,
you, the moon with the feet of the river,
you, clumsy wind,
you, bastard tree,
Crippled meat of two workmanlike wars,
you, quartered brother, butcher's boy,
too little for drinking money, too little
for burial, too little to cover,
you with that year that uses you,
1931 you,
you, one who is nothing but ten cords of wood
and two gnawed beds,
two dozen hammers, knives, zinc hooks,
bone brother, indentured soothsayer of veal,
you, a brain for now two sows
bowing down before him,
their provider, he who, whatever becomes of him, keeps
                                                 them secret
and boasts of his fatty virtue between his balls!

Morning

When my morning mixes with the morning
    of my friends,

when your sleep kills the face of the sea,
    the pestilential face of the spiritless summer,

when you wake up, drayman, doppelgänger
    of my inflamed eyes,

and the villages take on the colours of noon,
    my lie contemplates Shelley's corpse

in the sweet fragrance of the city of hills—
    weeping over my inconsolable days.

Description of a Family (II)

Horse traders, farmers, grenadiers,
     a senior officer, a cardinal ... and annual figures greater
                             than the earth
of the old dead, who walk through dark passageways,
     vaults, who talk of nothing, who only admonish you
and no writing and all great writing
     and no books where there are only books ... Now the
                        villages take revenge
and ask, what are you and when and where ...
     That, which is not,
which can no longer be as well,
     which the frost says, which the forests beyond you say ...
And what you say, which does not concern them at all,
     and what you are, no one is willing to understand any more,
and what you drink no one is willing to buy you ...
     Horse traders, farmers, grenadiers,
a senior officer, a cardinal ... the words,
     which mean nothing to one who is nothing ...
The doors black,
     you still know no names,
the cockle stoves do not burn for you,
     the beds too,
and your father's dog, which will tear you apart ...

(1963)

Now in Spring

Now in spring
   I can no longer understand
the language of the fields
   and the dead watch me
with their enormous eyes
   and the wheat churns
and the river talks to me of heaven . . .
   Where children laugh,
for my land is stranger
   than all the nations
of the earth.

(1963)

The Insane

The hunchback with the water pail,
her with the braids all wild,
the nun tails white, the birds
black on a green image,

him with the forefinger
on his bloody forehead,
him with the yellow rope
climbing the cherry tree,

him with the black frock,
him with the yellow pants,
him with the girl's face,
him with the red rose,

him with the hazelnut stick,
him with the crying,
him with the goat bleat,
with the bandy legs,

her with the red hair,
her with the long tongue,
her with the turnip knife,
with the bad lungs,

her with the white veil
in the black door,
her with the long neck,
her with the cropped ear,

her with the rosary, with
the apples, the pears,
them with the yellow-white
vacant brows,

her with the fear of the doctor,
her with the cabbage-leaf hat,
her letting her blood drip
in the water of the pond,

her walking through
the garden on tiptoes, her with
her eyes
mowing the meadow,

her with her hair
tied to the fence
wanting to scream,
her covered with scratches,

her coming from the chapel,
her looking from the window,
her with the rusty sickle
cutting off the flower tops,

her with the black stocking,
her on the hay wagon,
him, who those with red
skirts beat outside the barn,

her running from the kitchen
with the soup pot,
her with the mourning cap
on a red head,

her with the white
coat, with the blue
christening bow around the neck,
them looking in the apple basket,

them on the green milk
floating down in the dusk,
them in the black forest
going under in the cold night . . .

(1963)

In silva salus

King: Though yet of Hamlet our dear brother's death the memory be green, and that is us befitted . . .

I ask the death's head in the forest
    for my father . . .
Father . . .
    the moon hangs like a corpse
between two treetops, so
    as to deceive me . . . there
is the spine, through which the wind whistles . . .
    Father, you have killed
my heart . . . two feet without boots,
    a rusty belt buckle
reflected in the pond . . .
    Two steps away
your rotten shoulder strap . . .
    How shall I hear through the undergrowth
what you give me for an answer,
    where so many voices are?
I ask the death's head in the forest
    for my father . . .

(1963)

To H.W. (II)

Three thousand years after the father
    I died upon the hill, the wind,

a charred skull, me, the north,
    the alphabet of Virgil, the discourses of great farmers,

three thousand years after the father
    I went through my land, feeling sick,

me freezing in September's beds.

(1963)

No Tree (I)

A reason for John Donne

No tree
will understand you,
no forest,
no river,

no frost,
not ice, not snow,
no winter, you,
no me,

No storm wind
on high, no grave,
not East, not West,
no weeping, woe—
no tree . . .

(1963)

Two Beer Bottles and an Ice Stock

Two beer bottles
    and an ice stock, what does
my exalted brain say to that,
    my exalted teacher,
Sunday's sermonizer in the prison pulpit.

Two beer bottles
    and a pair of earmuffs
against the hunger's sky . . . what's that
    to me, that I
better not listen,
    foot-word wretch, chin-count cheater,
you damned hog-gelder of a winter!

Two beer bottles
    and an ice stock
and the lullabyist of death . . . why have
    a word with me where I know nothing,
a butcher's apron votary,
    a chimney sweep,
a high-and-mighty starset gendarme?

(1963)

Kitzlochklamm

For Rafael Alberti

The farmer in the black field
    in which the birds settle . . .
The white church tower. The woman with the child
    still goes raspberry picking.

Dusty faces. The warm wind
    descends where the firs
slowly turn brown. The clouds pull
    on the bells of the firs.

Workers stagger home in the rain,
    the book-bag children stand
down at the station. The waters plunge
    wildly down from on high.

At the inn, the railwayman taken aback
    trumps with the jack of bells.
Then from the forest come two dead men
    under an umbrella.

(1963)

Pain

A woman's coffin,
    what kind of silence is that?

A child's coffin,
    what kind of reward is that?

What is that then in the front hall?
    What is that in the branches?

What is that for the father?
    What is that for the son?

(1963)

Memory of the Dead Mother

A white face lies in the morgue, you can pick it up
and bring it home, but it's better that you bury it quickly in
                                                    her parents' plot,
before the winter sets in and that beautiful smile of your
                                        mother gets covered in snow.

(1963)

Afterword | JAMES REIDEL

I wrote a lot of poems, which I thought were better than those of Rilke, Trakl and everyone else . . .

Thomas Bernhard

3,000 pages of poetry still lie in his archive. There Bernhard reveals himself in every one of them as a pathos-drunken dilettante.

Raimund Fellinger, *Die Welt*

Beginning with the earliest poems and ending on the last, one could almost be reading a mental breakdown in a verse play and then slowly self-medicating himself into mental health. There is that. Then there is the uptick in their difficulty. Like the cautionary wording and gruesome images found on today's cigarette packs, a label might be placed on this book, a 'note of caution in regard to the difficulty of these poems', as one reviewer put it, for the poet seems to 'forbid any sweeping thesis'. The poems are 'always beyond analysis [. . .] permeated with silvery spun conundrums'.[1] And for these reasons and the dismay they still elicit,

---

1 Peter von Matt, review of Thomas Bernhard, *Gesammelte Gedichte* [Collected Poems] (Volker Bohn ed.) (Frankfurt am Main: Suhrkamp, 1991), *Frankfurter Allgemeine Zeitung* (10 August 1991).

Thomas Bernhard's poetry is still treated as an outlier to the work that brought him fame in German and in translation. Bernhard's novels, such as *Frost* (1963), *Gargoyles* (*Verstörung*, 1967), *The Lime Works* (*Das Kalkwerk*, 1970) and *Correction* (*Korrektur*, 1979), and plays such as *Heldenplatz* (1988), have firmly established his reputation, that of a far more irascible Kafka. (And like Kafka, Bernhard's challenging fiction has been made more accessible by the latest literary modality: the graphic novel.) In these works, he kept perfecting his virtually monologic narratives that dealt with themes of madness, self-destruction and self-creation. Intensely wrought, his fiction and theatre ultimately and ironically dealt with the impossibility of achieving perfection—especially artistic and intellectual perfection—and the enormity of failure and its grim and commensurate *comedy*. Not only was it limited to the individual but it also extended to the collective, in the form of the state, his penultimate antagonist next to God.

This peculiar relationship quickly marked every step in Bernhard's becoming the writer he was and, I would say, ended his career as a poet. His first published works in the early 1950s were poems, and he devoted a little over a decade to becoming not just any poet but the most important Austrian poet, the one who would achieve *fame* in the way he meant it, which is not celebrity per se but a matter of existential survival. That is, one's presence is granted, seen and validated by others—to experience *thereness*, what Heidegger called *Dasein*. This is a distinction, especially in reading Bernhard in English translation, which has to be recalled for he invokes *fame* (*Ruhm*) over and over again.

In his poems, the individual-as-Bernhard and Austria come to be ruthlessly and theatrically pathologized. Although he never waves that nation's red-and-white flag, Bernhard, the anti-poet and anti-patriot, cannot help but reveal that his country looms large in the world. When the 'programme' of his poetry becomes that of his fiction, Bernhard's stature virtually overshadows, eclipses and emigrates from his origins. And part of this programme, it seems, is the 'Unknown Bernhard', as one reviewer saw Bernhard's volume of collected poems, a book not unlike those obsessive and unfinished works and those obsessive and unrealized geniuses of his fiction.

Nicolaas Thomas Bernhard was born on 9 February 1931 in Heerlen, Netherlands. His mother, Herta Bernhard (1904–1950), had conceived him in the Austrian town of Henndorf am Wallersee during a brief affair with a carpenter named Alois Zuckerstätter (1905–1940). When Zuckerstätter learnt that Herta was pregnant, he set his parents' house on fire and left for Germany. Knowing that she would shame herself and her family, Herta, too, left Austria to wait out her pregnancy in a Dutch home for unwed and expectant women and girls, where she earned her room and board by subjecting herself and her unborn child to student midwives.

Bernhard wrote in one short story that the happiest time of his life had been the one year he spent as an infant in the Netherlands, and that his troubled childhood began as soon as he and his mother returned to Austria in 1932. At various times, the young Bernhard lived in Vienna, Henndorf, Salzburg and elsewhere. He never had a sense of a permanent home or any certainty about his background. He owed his surname to his grandmother's first husband, for she became pregnant with Herta before she married her lover and second husband, Bernhard's maternal grandfather, Johannes Freumbichler (1881–1949), an Austrian *Heimatschrift-steller*, a regional author who wrote genre novels of peasant life and types. And Bernhard never met his real father. Zuckerstätter had other reasons than just avoiding paying for child care. He had a reputation for being a troublemaker, a drunk and a man with communist leanings. The law fell harder on his kind in fascist Austria—and he would have been under surveillance. (A police report states that Zuckerstätter had returned to the Salzburg area in 1932, where he was involved in a barroom shouting match with local Nazis and subsequently fled back to Germany.[2])

In 1936, Herta Bernhard married Emil Fabjan, a hair-dresser and her young son's tutor. From this time, Bernhard should have experienced a semblance of family life. But his stepfather never officially adopted the boy; and having siblings, a half-brother and sister, meant less attention from a mother who had long blamed the unplanned birth of her first child for her troubled life. As Thomas matured, the disparagement only increased as the boy's resemblance to his reprobate father grew more obvious.

Following the *Anschluss*, the Fabjan family moved to Traunstein, Bavaria. There Bernhard suffered being the lone

---

2 See Christian Strasser, 'Antisemitismus am Wallersee' [Antisemitism at the Wallersee], *Der Geschmack der Vergänglichkeit: jüdische Sommerfrische in Salzburg* [The Taste of Impermanence: A Jewish Summer Resort in Salzburg] (Robert Kriechbaumer ed.) (Vienna: Böhlau, 2002), p. 144.

Austrian boy in a German school. He wept at being forced to go. The trauma of being bullied at school resulted in bedwetting accidents which his mother tried to curb by hanging his urine-soiled sheets in the window for the townspeople to see. Despite these and other enormous difficulties, Bernhard exhibited a precocious intelligence that his maternal grandfather mentored. When the Fabjan family returned to the Salzburg area in the early 1940s, Johannes Freumbichler assumed a greater role and cultivated the young Bernhard as the heir to his intellectual talents as well as his enormous reservoir of disappointments and frustration after seeing one of his novels finally win an important Austrian prize one year and becoming banned—along with its author—the next. Ironically, this enormous setback meant that Freumbichler could give Bernhard the attention he needed along with a valuable education he would get from no university—his grandfather's vast store of literary experience and a library of German and world literature and philosophy that fed the boy's interest in Goethe, Schopenhauer, Montaigne and such exotic Americans as William Cullen Bryant and Walt Whitman.

Despite being able to pore over great books and being schooled by Freumbichler's knowledge—and resentments—Bernhard's depressions and behaviour became an ever greater burden for his mother. After having sought out his paternal grandfather and given a photograph of his father, Herta snatched it from him and burnt it in the fireplace. She also enrolled her son in a boarding school for troubled youth, where he once more was traumatized, wet his bed and endured the ritual display of his yellow sheets. Eventually,

Bernhard was allowed to return to Salzburg and was enrolled in an elite high school. The Nazi faculty, however, made school a torment for him, as did the bombing raids of the Eighth Air Force in 1944. Bernhard's memoirs recount the daily horrors of corpses piled up in the streets of Salzburg, of peering inside a basement full of dead railwaymen and of seeing a child's severed hand in the rubble. In the autumn of 1945, the teenage Bernhard attempted suicide and dropped out of school.

Fortunately, Upper Austria had been occupied by the Americans, and Bernhard returned to Freumbichler's regimen of proper books. Life, however, proved grim in postwar Austria. Compelled by the limited means of his family, Bernhard apprenticed himself to a grocer and found the work of unloading barrels and crates and being with ordinary working people from butchers to farmhands to be an antidote to his previous life of being a lonely and neglected child. His employer, a man who enjoyed classical music, had heard Bernhard's fine baritone voice and helped him pay for voice lessons at the Mozarteum.

The grocery store, however, proved to be injurious to his health. The bad air, the mould and, finally, working in a rainstorm brought a bout of pleurisy in 1947. Too sick and weak for work, Bernhard began to write his first poems over the next two years, leading up to his confinement at the Grafenhof tuberculosis sanatorium in the remote town of Sankt Veit im Pongau—where he contracted the disease as well as suffered the abuse of the staff and other patients. According to his memoir, on the eve of his going into

Grafenhof, when his mother began a long battle with uterine cancer, he read her some of his poems. 'She wept—we both wept,' he wrote of the experience. 'I embraced her, then packed my case and vanished. Would I ever see her again? She was *forced* to listen to my poems—I gave her no choice. I was sure they were good. They were compositions of a desperate eighteen-year-old to whom they seemed to be all he had left in the world.'[3]

In 1949 and 1951, respectively, Bernhard learnt of the deaths of his beloved grandfather and mother from newspaper obituaries. That neither his stepfather nor any other family member had written to him became a great source of resentment. He suffered his mother's loss keenly and his poetry is tinged with that. But once more the kindness of a stranger interceded. Hedwig Stavianicek (1894–1984), a widow of a former director of Grafenhof and more than thirty-seven years his senior, had been charmed by his attempts to recover his singing voice. Frau Stavianicek also discovered that young Bernhard had both literary talent and aspirations. Eventually, she became his virtual guardian and patroness, giving him a place to live after he was discharged from the sanatorium as well as financial support, for he could hardly return to the stepfamily from which he had estranged himself.

'Tante' (Auntie), as Bernhard called Frau Stavianicek, became the only woman in his life, and though his poems betray an interest in women, he was, whether hetero- or

---

3 Thomas Bernhard, *Gathering Evidence: A Memoir* (David McLintock trans.) (New York: Alfred A. Knopf, 1985), p. 291.

homosexual, ultimately neither. Like his grandfather Freumbichler, he preferred his purely intellectual pursuits, such as reading and rereading all of Pascal, Montaigne, Goethe, Schopenhauer and Wittgenstein. He also involved himself in the literary life of Austria as the occupation came to an end and the republic was restored, working as a journalist for the *Demokratisches Volksblatt*, Salzburg's socialist party newspaper, turning in reviews and cultural pieces. Bernhard also continued to find his voice and way, writing new poems—in step with the renaissance in German verse during the postwar period. Poetry, too, had an immediacy of composition which appealed to Bernhard and other younger writers who also saw poetry as not just the first stage in a 'real' literary career of being a writer of scale and scope, say a novelist, playwright or both. To be a poet would not only be enough, it would protest such a hierarchy, be radical, violate expectations, indeed, exhibit those very qualities found in Bernhard's verse. Lastly, poetry provided a long-needed voice for the suppression of the Nazi period and to express the feelings of its aftermath. Thus, Bernhard easily published his poems and these early successes pointed him in the direction he took in the 1950s.

Like other postwar Austrian poets, Bernhard looked to Georg Trakl as a model. The pathos and melancholy of Trakl's verse not only predicated Austria's downfall in the early years of the twentieth century but also anticipated subsequent generations and permutations of that downfall being a continuous process. Trakl, too, provided a source of nostalgia and refuge of dark but enchanting landscapes and folkways which elided the banal realities of the Hapsburg Empire, the disastrous First Republic and the Austro-Fascist and Nazi regimes. In this way, Bernhard's earliest poems evoke this postcard, *Sound of Music* Salzburg and its environs. Gradually, however, Bernhard moves—or *transgresses*—from his 'innocent pastoral poems' towards 'a landscape of sorrow [...] a cemetery of fantasy and desire'.[4] This is the Austria Bernhard described as 'beautiful on the surface but horrifying underneath', which required 'a form of lyrical self-exorcism'. His 'problem' with Austria, of how he came to be both from Austria and born apart from it, became the heart of his poetry, its *Herkunftcomplex*—its complex over one's origins, one's background, one's home. It forced his pretty and ironic 'blissful year' poems back to what Germans and Austrians called the postwar time—*Jahr Null*.[5]

In 1957, Bernhard's first book of poems appeared. *Auf der Erde und in der Hölle* (*On Earth and in Hell*, 1957) had to have come as a validation of Bernhard's talents—but it did not come easy. The publisher, Otto Müller-Verlag, adhered to the tastes and standards of the firm's mentor, the venerable Ludwig von Ficker. As the grand old man of Austrian literature, whose career went back to the early twentieth century, when he had befriended and mentored Trakl, von Ficker's endorsement was requisite for any young Austrian poet. How much so can be measured by Bernhard's

---

4 Paola Bozzi, 'Homeland, Death, and Otherness in the Early Lyrical Work' in Matthias Konzett (ed.), *A Companion to the Works of Thomas Bernhard* (Rochester, NY: Camden House, 2002), p. 75.

5 Bernhard, *Gathering Evidence*, p. 82.

attempts to win the coveted Trakl Prize in Poetry, an award juried by von Ficker and other leading members of Austria's literati which included publication of the winning entry. Bernhard had submitted manuscripts for the prize between 1952 and 1956. Although his entries were often praised, they always missed the mark. Naturally, he suffered over their rejection and any criticism of his style and content. In 1955, he complained bitterly to his friend, the Austrian poet Christine Lavant, who responded, 'No matter what, Thomas, I beg you not to give up on yourself. You can very much be, you are a poet and you will always remain one . . .'.[6] Bernhard took the advice and once more submitted poems from *On Earth and in Hell* in a second attempt to win the Trakl Prize. Although his entry was among the finalists and praised by von Ficker himself, it was passed over once more In the end, however, Otto Müller funded the publication of *On Earth and in Hell* with another stipend.

Although he had not won the Trakl Prize, Bernhard saw himself as taking up where Trakl left off. To his critics, he seemed to channel Trakl to the point where some called him Trakl's 'voice impressionist'. Carl Zuckmayer, the renowned German screenwriter, and his wife Alice saw Bernhard as an original. Both knew Bernhard's maternal grandfather during the 1930s, when the Zuckmayers lived in Henndorf. After the war, when the Zuckmayers returned from exile, Alice urged Bernhard to publish his poems. Her husband also shared her enthusiasm and praised Bernhard's

6 Christine Lavant to Thomas Bernhard, quoted in Raimund Fellinger, 'Kommentar' [Commentary] in Thomas Bernhard, *Gedichte* [Poems] (Berlin: Suhrkamp, 2015), p. 403.

first book as 'perhaps the greatest discovery I have made in the last decade of our literature', with 'the distinctive features of the great modern poetry . . . the rhythm of an entire nation'.

Although there were few reviews, Bernhard felt himself to be on the same course as other rising young poets of the German language, among them the Austrian poet Ingeborg Bachmann. For her part, she welcomed the debut, but only tepidly, writing a friend, after he had sent her *On Earth and in Hell*, that 'He—Bernhard—is already there— with all the drive to write poems and yet not in the poems themselves.'[7]

A year later, in 1958, he published his second book of verse, *In Hora Mortis* (*At the Hour of Death*). Reading like a devotional meditation owing to his near-death experiences from lung disease, Bernhard had written a spiritual book in dispirited times. However, his dialogue with God, his testimony of faith, is about its absurdity. Indeed, Bernhard's incessant lamentation (*Klagerei*) reveals the depth of a despair that is behind his famously reflexive antipathy for the Church and clergy. These poems and virtually every poem by Bernhard seem cast in suffering and expressed with a kind of penitential psalmistry as though from another time and place far more remote than Upper Austria. Indeed, they have all the bearing of the Book of Job and, like Job, a

---

7 Quoted in Thomas Bernhard and Peter Hamm, *Sind Sie gern böse? 'Ein Nachtgespräch zwischen Thomas Bernhard und Peter Hamm im Hause Bernhard in Ohlsdorf 1977* [Do They Like Being Evil? A Night Conversation between Thomas Bernhard and Peter Hamm in Bernhard's House in Ohlsdorf, 1977] (Berlin: Suhrkamp, 2011), p. 7.

man eager to drink up scorning like water given the course his poetry took from this point.

In Hora Mortis was followed by another long collection, *Unter dem Eisen des Mondes* (*Under the Iron of the Moon*, 1958), in which Bernhard more fully waxed into being an 'archivist of the negative', a 'disappointed metaphysician' whose goal is a comedy that is hardly divine—'that everything is ridiculous in the face of death'.[8] His poetry became unrelenting in its grimness, a 'realm of mourning, black suns and the moon of the dead [. . .] a world after the abolishment of the world [. . .] in a state of dissolution. It is a world of broken identities and fragments of abandoned cultures'. With three books of poems already published by 1958, Bernhard had certainly validated himself as an important younger poet, one 'acutely aware of the need to recall the grand epic tradition and hence his implicit references to Vergil, Dante, Hölderlin and T. S. Eliot'.[9] Bernhard's despair must have seemed to readers, critics and editors only balanced by an ambition to get it all on paper. However, what is quoted here came later, for despite the energy Bernhard put into this poetry, he saw very few book reviews and like critical attention. His iron moon refused to rise.

In the late 1950s, Bernhard studied acting at the Mozarteum and performed in its productions of Jean Anouilh's *Antigone* and Klaus Gmeiner's *The Enchanted Forest*. Given the theatrical quality of his poems—they are

---

8 Bozzi, 'Homeland, Death, and Otherness', pp. 80–1.
9 Rüdiger Görner, 'Bernhard's Notion of Weltbezug' in Konzett, *A Companion,* p. 92.

almost best read as dramatic speeches—such a vocation would seem a natural course for the young poet. Indeed, the theatre's influence is unmistakable in the long and dialogic poem *Ave Vergil* (*Ave Virgil*, 1981), written in late 1959 and early 1960. A collection of semi-autobiographical fragments—'various stations of an epic' as one critic called it—the poem resembles Dylan Thomas's radio play *Under Milk Wood* which Bernhard had read and admired.

Between 1958 and 1961, Bernard prepared several new manuscripts for publication. The most ambitious was initially titled *Mysterium der Karwoche* (*The Mystery of Holy Week*) and submitted to Otto Müller in mid-1959. The editorial opinion of the nearly 150 pages of new poems, culled from the hundreds that Bernhard had written, was mixed. His friend Gerhard Fritsch praised the manuscript as an 'exceptional book of verse'. While his instincts told him that on the whole it was stronger and more original than many other collections by other poets, he felt that its value would be enhanced if Bernhard might revise the book with the object of achieving more economy, concentrating on their form (become increasingly sprawling with long lines that more resembled prose) and clarifying their content (for Bernhard's verse had become ever more private, to the point of being inaccessible to readers unless they knew him personally). Von Ficker agreed: while Bernhard's new poems struck him as very alive, personal and intense, striking at the 'centre' of every kind of absurdity that life offered, he felt that the self-pitying and defamatory passages were too excessive. Nevertheless, Bernhard had made an 'edifice' that deserved awe, even reverence, both harrowing and disturbing to read. He was, nevertheless, a rising and important young writer and von Ficker felt he should be helped out of the dead end of any unreasonable demands from either himself or his editors. Although Bernhard tried to rework the poems to satisfy Fritsch and von Ficker, the results were all the more 'exclamations of self-pity'.

Undaunted, and unconvinced by Otto Müller's editors about the direction of his verse, Bernhard sent the manuscript to Germany's most prestigious literary publisher, S. Fischer Verlag, in the spring of 1961. Fischer had published his ballet libretto *die rosen der einöde* (*the rose of the desert*, 1959) and Bernhard felt he could now risk the good relationship he had developed with the editor Richard Moissl. Instead, Bernhard only exhausted Moissl's good will and patience, for he had yet another book in mind. Inspired by Virginia Woolf's *Orlando* and her description of England's winter of 1609–10, the 'Great Frost', Bernhard informed Moissl of the necessity of changing the title of his manuscript to *Frost* (version A/B). However, the conceit, the imagery, the key words of 'cold', 'frost' and an omnipresent 'winter' were hardly present. Thus, in November, and to Moissl's surprise, Bernhard submitted an entirely new manuscript (version C). 'You will not recognize it,' Bernhard wrote to the editor, 'now it is monumental and a river that even capsizes me.'[10] He also intensified everything that editors had found good (or bad) about the earlier version, including the undulant self-pity and grief, the verbal *art brut* (in the way the poems seemed like the work of a butcher boy). And the voice in

---

10 Thomas Bernhard to Richard Moissl, quoted in *Gedichte*, p. 426.

the poems savaged postwar Austria with even more acerbity. In virtually every poem, Bernhard's had at last truly crossed over into a kind of *total anti-poetry*. His prose-like, voluminous, concatenated lyrics form a catalogue of despair and misrelation vis-à-vis the audience, whether it is Bernhard himself, his publishers or the reading public in general. In effect, he had become *bardic*—to borrow from the late Terrence Des Pres' meaning—he had become a people's poet, charged with *dispraising* the conduct of a nation as much as finding empathy for it. 'I am,' Bernhard writes in a late poem, 'in the highest balcony / in every one of songs for a weary people, / for them and for my and for my certifiably insane earth' (p. 325). From such a cheap seat, in the rows of the 'gods' to use theatre parlance, Bernhard still wanted fame and renown for his poems, for his vast, misshapen and misbegotten Austrian realm of words, and to be seen looking down—on the lost Austrian empire, republics and Nazi province. Therein lies the black comedy, which is detectable in the poems and so obvious in his novels, plays and interviews, his cosmic joke.

Moissl did not see any of this—nor the inherent absurdity and comedy in its oldest form, the infliction of pain by others in Bernhard's new poetry—which, in translation and hindsight given Bernhard's later writing, fully evinced. Indeed, one of his readers had already recommended that version A/B not be published for all the same reasons which von Ficker had, adding that the inference that Bernhard as the tramp and 'lamenteer' was simply a pose. In a tactful rejection letter, Moissl told Bernhard that *On Earth and in Hell*, his first book, was much better and that *Frost* really only covered the same ground. Moissl wanted to know why Bernhard was so obsessed with defaming everyone but himself. Although S. Fischer was a publisher receptive to experimental literature, the editor was still mindful of the sensibilities of average readers—and Bernhard's poetry surely would have tested their patience, intellect and credulity. His image of Austria as this polar dystopia, as much emblematic of Germany, would have been unintelligible, cognitive dissonance in the climate of the Economic Miracle and that other 'miracle', of distance from the Nazi period.

Bernhard, who saw the final version of *Frost* his 'Fleurs de mal', was devastated and refused to go back to the earlier manuscript. 'I cannot tamper with it,' he wrote, 'I am certain that every word in my manuscript is a reality through which I have lived from getting nowhere, but that is a prerequisite!'[11] In the months that followed, Bernhard published some of the poems he had intended for the *Frost* manuscripts in anthologies of new German verse. A handful appeared in English for the first time in a New Directions anthology of contemporary German poetry. In 1962, he privately printed the long allegorical, side-by-side poems *Die Irren   Die Häftlinge* (*The Insane   The Inmates*). But he had stopped writing poems by this time and consigned a decade of work to the catchall of simply being 'literary development'.

Bernhard wrote his first novel—and perhaps boldly—gave it the repurposed title *Frost*, which was published to much critical acclaim in 1963. Over the next two decades, he

11 Bernhard to Moissl, quoted in *Gedichte*, pp. 426–7.

established himself as one of Austria's leading novelists with a prodigious list of titles, and answering his fame with becoming a kind of public recluse whose pronouncements often infuriated his countrymen—his critiques of every facet of Austrian society were relentless and ranged from the Church and politics (especially the socialist government) to the country's Nazi past and anti-Semitism and were least sparing when it came to Austria's cultural and literary establishment. His novels and his plays during the 1980s, especially *Heldenplatz* (Heroes' Square, 1988), earned him the epitaph of a *Nestbeschmutzer*, he who shits in the nest.

Throughout his controversial career, Bernhard gave much thought to his poems, how they were received—and rejected. To his friend and editor at Suhrkamp, Günther Busch, he lamented the fate of his first book, *On Earth and in Hell*. 'I'm sorry now that these poems, my most successful,' he wrote, 'are totally lost and forgotten.'[12] Years later, he wrote on the flyleaf of his copy of *Under the Iron of the Moon* that it still pleased him 'very much'.[13] And though he wrote no more poetry himself, he served as a poetry consultant for his publisher at the height of his career as a prose writer. In 1970, he selected poems by Trakl for the Bibliothek Suhrkamp series. He also recommended poems by Ingeborg Bachman for the same series and assumed the

---

12 Thomas Bernhard to Günther Busch, 2 June 1967, quoted in Thomas Bernhard and Siegfried Unseld, *Der Briefwechsel* [The Correspondence] (Raimund Fellinger, Martin Huber and Julia Ketterer eds) (Berlin: Suhrkamp, 2009), p. 58n3.
13 Quoted in Thomas Bernhard, *Gesammelte Gedichte* [Collected Poems] (Volker Bohn ed.) (Frankfurt am Main: Suhrkamp, 1991), p. 335.

editorship of a selection of Christine Lavant's work in the early 1980s.

During that same decade, Bernhard began to reclaim what was to him a fundamental part of his *oeuvre* and legacy and which so many critics imagined that he had abandoned. He revised the order and content of *On Earth and in Hell* with the intent of publishing again. He issued chapbooks of *Ave Virgil, In Hora Mortis* and *The Insane   The Inmates.* He even wrote a 'last' poem for *Die Zeit* to mark New Year's Day, 1982. Ultimately, he made provisions in his will for a collected edition of only his published poems, the first of his works to appear following his death in February 1989. A quarter of a century later, in 2015, his literary estate allowed for an expanded volume to accompany the first edition of his collected works. The renderings in this book are drawn from those two editions, including the Appendix of poems from the *Frost* manuscripts which Bernhard had attempted to embargo from any publication or translation until 2059— the maximum period allowed by Austrian law.

Cognizant of that, I made the editorial decision to place the *Frost* poems outside of the collected poems proper. They follow this afterword (as does a 'final' outlier poem Bernhard wrote at the request of *Die Zeit* in 1981).

Those who attempt to translate the works of Bernhard must reconcile themselves to his low opinion of translation. Where some Austrian writers might hope for the best and a handsome profit—I am thinking here of Franz Werfel, whose work I have translated and whose bestsellers could almost be seen as exports and sources of foreign capital for Austria's troubled economy during the Depression— Bernhard found the endeavour of translation both annoying and pointless. To him, a translation was 'a different book' because a 'translation is impossible', which is to say, an *impossible book* with 'awful covers' and 'weirdly different' titles.[14] Indeed, he would see such a book as this to be a *Verirrung*, an aberration.

What I have done is not unlike those monuments of artistic failures described again and again in his novels and short stories. If I have succeeded in anything, it is to show that the programme in his fiction could not have come into existence without the poetry and Bernhard's raw, visceral attachment to it. (One need only look at how many times he uses the word *entrails*.) I quite understand what he means in the note that ends one of his manuscripts from 1960: '[A]fter so many years / disconsolate, dreadful / aberration!!!'[15] Was Bernhard acknowledging an achievement? A monstrosity? Or, perhaps, a poetry *of* monstrosity?

That said about Bernhard on translation and his 'translation' of himself into a poet, into verse, I discovered his work in the late 1970s and 80s through some of the finest literary translations I have ever read and which inspired me to learn the exacting process myself. There were still works by Bernhard which I wanted to read, including the poems in this volume, so I taught myself with his work. After

---

14 This and the following quotes are from Werner Wögerbauer, 'Thomas Bernhard for Life' [transcript of a 1986 interview]. Available at: www.sightandsound.com (11 December 2006).

15 Quoted in *Gedichte*, p. 439.

some years, Princeton University Press published my earlier rendering of *In Hora Mortis* and *Under the Iron of the Moon* in its Lamont series. Its lunar and Traklesque cover was quite fitting and the book was one of three finalists for the PEN translation prize for 2006. For Bernhard, it would have been all wrong, no matter how hard one tried to approximate his work, correct one's errors and revise and revise. 'A piece of music is played the same the world over, using the written notes,' he said, expanding his disdain for his work in translation, 'but a book would always have to be played in German, in my case. With my orchestra!'

With those watchwords to contemplate, what could be more of an orchestral and personal work than Bernhard's complete poems? All I can say here is that he, at least, haunts every word in English which I have chosen for my notes, for my orchestra. This comes with the ultimate revelation, too, which I hope one can hear in the music you read here, that Bernhard remained a poet in the end as much as he did at the beginning.

Paranoia?

In *Hamburg* when I
suddenly felt hungry,
I walked into a restaurant
and ordered myself,
having arrived from Krakow,
a pork sausage with dumplings
and a half pint of beer.
On a journey through Slovakia
my stomach felt empty.
I chatted with the innkeeper,
he said, the Polish Jews
should have all been killed
without exception.
He was a Nazi.

In *Vienna* I walked inside the Hotel Ambassador
and ordered myself a cognac,
a French one naturally, I said,
maybe a Martell
and chatted with a painter,
who continually claimed himself
to be an artist
and who knew what art was,

not even the rest of the world knew
what art was,
as it soon turned out,
he was a Nazi.

In *Linz* I walked into the Café Draxelmayer
for a small coffee with cream
and spoke with the headwaiter
about the football match between Rapid and LASK
and the headwaiter said,
the Rapids all deserved to be gassed,
Hitler would have more to do today
than in his own lifetime,
and as it soon turned out
he was a Nazi.

In *Salzburg* I met my former religion professor
who told me to my face
that my books
and, in general, everything that I have written until now,
were trash,
but today you can publish the greatest trash,
he said, in a time like this,
which is nothing but trash,
in the Third Reich I could not have published
any of my books, he said
and in so many words told me that I was a pig
and a fraudulent dog
and he bit into his baloney sandwich
and with both hands put on his cassock

and stood up and left.
He is a Nazi.

I received a postcard from *Innsbruck* yesterday
with the Golden Roof,
on which was written without giving any reason:
Those such as you deserve to be gassed! Just wait!
I read the card several times
and felt afraid for myself.

(1982)

Appendix

Frost

(Manuscript C)

1931

Leave me alone, you, 1931, you, leave me alone!
Pull on my rags! Leave me alone, cretin!
What did I gulp down for you? How? What? You?
Go to hell, you, bastard, district inspector!

Cretin! Boothead! Up, march—march!
March straight! March! 1931, from head to ass!

On the Kapuzinerberg

                              looking down
The foliage is the music for my dead feet,
for my lungs in bondage. From a thousand scraps torn apart,
the afternoon sleeps inside me,
a wooden post is my rotten silent partner

over the roofs of the city, over the black
river. On the bridges cross the afflicted
of the mediocrity into the city's other half,
hornet swarms of rectitude,

self-seeking dogs with rotten lofty brows,
miserable card-file keepers, the federal security police
with *The Elective Affinities* of Goethe on the brain,
a page torn from 'There was a king in Thule . . . '

The rain mutilates their spitefulness
on the ruined square, which the fountain
defiled in the racket of the brass band.
The storm wind crops their earlobes

and speaks of the insane acts of a hurried existence,
a parolee out of prison yesterday, who

like his brother the last night at the station[,]
slept between two bottles of beer.

These religions stupefy the people,
have sway over a pathetic race
of catarrh carriers, consumptives,
provincial intellectual Pharisees,

when the cold erupts in their testicles and chests
with that crying over the stacks of dead.

Fools and Those Mad

I attach myself to fools and those mad with torment,
those, the ones who hound me in the beer hall, on posters,
plank boards,
drifting through rivers, in the slaughterhouse darkness, those
I put on my tight trousers for and let drink
from my mercantile apathy, let sing songs!
You, my sirs, I say, you shameless women,
the world rears up on the crests of my hills, such that my
frostbite freezes,
that I am horrified of you!

I attach myself to fools and those mad,
with dismembered limbs I walk spring happy,
when the year shows me the flowers of its hands,
white, black as snow, its illegal panhandling turning nature
to a shred of misery inside me,
shattered heads, unburied dead watching me
and luring me down to where fear dies hard, deep under a
stone,
deep beneath the black smell of their lies! My brain is
killing me,
my sleep simply cornflower laden, and my shadows stretch
me before their laughter!

War's End

In the black leaves and rotting plaints I hear the funeral
march,
children shriek, crazed mothers, bloated, hunchbacked old
men
with spinning eyes, royal dignity spraying from ranks shot to
pieces!
Their tongues are dry from talking nonsense,
mauled by feeling sick to themselves, they win my
blubbering
there on the street; mirrors of bloody puddles
reveal the lies of their loneliness, a mindless beginning of
spring in stinking cities of ruins!

The streets scream murder! and blossom just like brass bands.
From the house-to-house insanity of brutal sanity
I feel numb and shameless
as my entrails are drawn out in the morning sun by the
instrument of this world,
I walk, renouncing the shadows, through the streets,
here, I pound skulls, here, a Republic!, here, eradicated
vermin,
here, a wonderful blackness!, here, feet!, here, the blackest
triumph of the catafalque: my people!

The world is a wasteland, deaf from misery, blind from hate
                                                and cold,
its brain now raped by the racket of a migratory bird. I go
                        not to waken my old friends,
sleep shall prepare them for the coming slaughter,
trumpet sweat shall brace up the heart and kidneys of sloppy
                                                Death,
who red and black shockingly forges plans on the wall,
incurably sick, for this poisoned earth.

Decay (I)

When the nights were not, I would be dead,
given how they howled in me, the dogs
making my brain and bones ring full of misery
from my stupid year, such that my hands tremble
and the grass must burn, the towers slit open
the belly of the sky, the rivers burst.

When the nights were not, I would be dead,
torn apart by the wheel along with the dead
in the leprosy of my agony. The fields hound, hiss
in the early winter leaves, my thoughts of nature splattering
                                                             black
on my face, the land, the city.

When the nights were not, I would be dead,
joints of slaughtered cattle, nothing but the whispers
of birds gone astray, restless worms,
dogs and cats,
a subterranean prominence of decay!

I Hear You Crouching in the Chapel

the ruined souls of the dogs at the bottom of the stream
with their crippled legs
for your splattered head,
for you fear of insane people.

Revolt

Bones break with my madness
eyes, ears, the black city, before me
walk these fine men, black, in long coats,
devilish creatures, ethereally craven,

on crutches, barking like the dogs
at the meat market, spelling out the rhymes
of this sour sky, now their death has
enormous teeth, these incurables

are not worth the tears, not one day
full of madness, folly, dripping from the
bloody neck of my morning bottle
and punching me in the mouth, for whom alone

the mountains now stand, the neglected ribs
of massive ridges, the sleeping vermin
of obscene autumns, the freezing shops
of butchers terminally ill, liar grenadiers

released from every city, from every river,
outrageously quiet . . . not one
train amputated face and backsides for them,
ruined them upon their first journey

to the desert sand below, to far up
in Lapland, before the Irish sheep,
mounds of snow, before their mournful heads,
who could have bleated inside their bowels

with the cold's apathy, an oratorical primal talent,
such that it fills the Atlantic with horror, sickens
not one snoutful from their gloom, hurrying it
with the urine of time, with that voluble

betrayal of the homeland ... lazy apprentice boys,
philosophers, meat cutters, philosophers,
convicts, truants, good-for-nothings
in the bellies of their wage boat eating their agony's

unremitting mercy,
their emaciated natures of female apathy ...

I travel through their churches by hand,
through their houses, forests, libraries,
such that these treasonous storms howl
down in the dust, down among the bones,
down in their grave of dissolute talents!

The Carrion

Mortified by what my brain thinks, it rots,
soon no shadow more of it will fall in this country,
soon too no dog will sniff it at daybreak . . .
no cockroach will kiss it on its most sensitive spot.

Tired of bread and meat and honey, fabricated
by one of the workless who found this creation,
it sleeps for millions of years without mercy
in the springtime moss, executed by the winter.

After the Verdict

After the verdict you descend
into the air poisoned by people,
you shut your mouth, the rhymes come
like the pollen . . . the besmirched jobsite

you try to explain to your brain . . .
Ask the wild man! He does not give
his name, one for him dwells in his face,
such that he freezes, such that his groaning

hastens the end of the world!
Black from hunger, your eyes are bleary good-luck charms
for the sordid twelve Omen Days of Christmas,
choker-downers of forced labour! In your trousers

the winter comes with its whiplashes
over the scaffold, turning your lungs black,
dragging you by your necks over the insanity
of men's limbs! Screams and curses

buckle your belts ever tighter . . . depreciated scrotums
hobbling in the sun, stumbling at twelve noon
on a truncated mound riven by thunder showers,
one which devours your snatches of conversation.

No One Knows You (II)

'My feast of joy is but a dish of pain'
Chidiock Tichborne, Spring 1586

No one knows you
and when you die
they slip on their coats
and bury you quickly.

Never forget that!

No one needs you
but when you die
they bang on the drum
and seal their lips.

Never forget that!

No one can hear you
and when you die
they trample your homesickness
back into the earth.

Never forget that!

No one kills you,
but when you die,
they spit in your beer mug
and you must pay.

The Dead Are Nothing

The dead are nothing, where the dead
were, nothing, where the dead
are, silence of lonely graves, the dead
without rest, nothing, no grave.

The dead are nothing, where white
the snow, rotten, raven black
the forest, where a tearful world
drinks a drowned cold, where the dead
were, nothing, mourn not,
not death, not sham.

The dead are nothing, where the dead
were, wintery, in that frost of graves
were the dead, a black night's nothing,
where decay still froze,
nothing, the dead, clear.

Vienna—Daybreak on the Karlsplatz (I)

Along with the stray dogs I am
    to heaven more despicable than hell,
rotting from the collarbone on down
    in the gigantic skull of my religions,
buried quick in the scenes
    of my desolation!

Snarled at by the storm wind,
    a bloody altar boy
of bawling October streets,
    dead already from laughing, sprawled in the whispers
of my ruined autumn.
    Suddenly, screamed at by the morning,
I stand in a forest of watchmen.

I Feel the Moon's Too Good (II)

Hamlet: That skull had a tongue in it and could
            sing once . . .

I feel the moon's too good
for greeting the Herr Gendarme,
I feel my hat's too tight,
I feel night sits at my feet.

I feel my brain's too dull,
I feel my head is unhinged,
I feel, my Herr Gendarme,
my heart is cut out whole too.

Who Comes into the House, the Frost

Who comes into the house, the frost
    and now I can
no longer sleep the night,
    given he who watches me closely,

and I walk away and I walk
    from the house,
thus does he claw out
    the last of my eyes

and suddenly I see,
    when the night dwindles,
the white winter,
    which already stands before me.

Winter (I)

The winter came without end
    in the main streets and on the squares
and drove man and dog together into a ball,
    such that the wind went astray in their heads
and the whole world was filled with howls against the harsh
        god.

    Alone on the street, I was witness to a hereafter no
        one summoned,
    they had no concern for my exhaustion, much less
        about for my bad brain,
    which swelled warped and sick from madness and
        folly, raged!

Not a single place in my verse did they realize betrayed me,
    betrayed to the dead, I was all clear about myself, no cold,
not the stanza of my forever humiliated fame!

My flesh crouched at their feet and I thought of their
        children
and I knew of their dissolute world, the cold
instilling them with my abuse! O . . .
I killed myself and my habitual ways in their houses,
    spitting from their palaces,
I founded my kingdom upon their kingdoms!

If I were ever from such a county, I would speak
                              their language
and I would cry their tears . . . until blamed across
                              the skies
in their agony, I am the one and only lord whom
                              they experience
and in my imperfection a laudable exception for all
                              time!

Insane with their backsliding I drive the holy winter
                              across the earth,
    and as the frost flees from me, I fear nothing
but the shadows of their love in my drowned breast.

Destruction of a Sonnet

Beneath the hands in the bleak sky,
    the water of the river, the black
firmament, in which the soul of death
    passes through neglected gardens.

Wind! The tremendous judge of my questions
    in the desecrated evening, whom you
no longer want me to hear, the flocks of birds
    above the bellowing of the stag

filling the valleys with utter darkess . . .
    Locked churches, frozen mountains,
the north's silence green and white.

A harbinger of March, a misappropriated slayer
    of cold, protects me and this time of invaders
from God and the mourning, ourselves!

Prison House (I)

Who digs in the graves of winter? Paws
    in the morgues? In the clear nights
through the guilty verdicts of a snow of giant skulls? Who
    runs their cups over for the dead, dialogues
of crucified frost? Stares at me
    forever wicked and crazy?

Creaking trees rule in the land
    above my prisoner's lot,
pounding stars, scenes of delirious tear-stained skies
    lead me downwards, the frozen keeper
of my ruins bores through me in that monarchy
    of my canonized crimes!

North and South

»Nous avons vu des astres
Et des flots; nous avons vu des sables aussi;
Et, malgré bien des chocs et d'imprévus désastres,
Nous nous sommes souvent ennuyés, comme ici.«

Baudelaire

I

I fled sick from the Irish cold
    into the dead streets of London, stood on Tower Bridge
and saw my country, the swarm of birds, the muted
    screams of black water flowing
    below, where no stream was my tears,
I found nothing there, nothing for my poor head frozen
                            stiff in a winter coat collar
    long frozen in a fat ship's belly, fleeing
every sea, a pig-headed sky's pimp
    shivering from truth, unastonished in the howling of
                            the storm . . .

II

The heat inflates my suffering
    on the battlements of Empedocles; the enormous choir
of war resistors shadowed
    the machine guns of puking infantrymen;

a main road of death, where the dead rotted from their
coffins,
great men waited, women went into labour in the noon
hour.
Bleary with decay I went searching through my half-sleep,
thoughts of my country, of the north's chilly grief
blanketed me,
down from the hills
they led me to an end.

Battle (I)

Do you hear the madness of my cold? Are you
    not shivering? The stiffened foot, which you must
watch in battle, like its older brother
    torn up in an evening sky boding dark marches
and like the sleep melting off my shaven skull?

    Do you hear the madness? A jog-trot of commanding
                           generals
through my brainsick blood, through a country's flesh made
                           of pain,
    through winter, in March ploughed into the front,
                     straining battle ranks
screaming? With impotence you fight a war and with heads
                     cemetery walls . . .

In the driving snow your mouth and thighs
    gape from weeping,
no king takes revenge on your hands,
    no error of one's grief, the broken curses
embroil you in night and howls, cup and horrors,
    such that your flesh falls exhausted from your soul
and stream-sharp tears sting upon the earth,
    which, startled in the moon, is tongue lashed
for an outrageous mistake,
    human madness betrayed, shattered from agony!

Against My Fellow Countrymen

Did I put forth the shadow of my hand? Did I put forth
my verdict on the field? My evil brain, the state of things
angry and empty, inflated with interest to pay off
in a thousand years? My temples are a match
to the sleep of kings, not the men behind them!

Hear me! My language perishes in their houses faster
than in the rivers, in the fields, meadows, on the crests
of sweating hills, those demonstrating how to kill
art to me on the square, on the wild boar's trail!

The meaning is scattered to me, my heart torn out, an
                                        apathetic sack
between my testicles, my land surveyor! Prisoners of the
                                        night,
my middlemen in the streets, rabid bridgeheads,
larded with royal titles, sprinkled over by princely losers!
My dirty fingers flash in their eyes and they suddenly see the
                                        glory
of their dead intrigues . . .
        Addicted to the murder of my mother, they stand
                around, with their hands in their pants pockets,
their taproom entrails torn apart by their idiocy, rotting
already in this insidious air!

Prison House (II)

Who digs in the graves of winter? Paws
in the morgues? Limps in clear nights
through guilty verdicts of a snow of giant skulls? Who
runs their cups over for the dead, these dialogues
of crucified frost? Stares at me out of the night,
forever wicked and crazy?

   The world is a prison house! A mouldering vortex
of creaking trees rule in the land above my prisoner's neck,
pounding stars, scenes of maniacal tear-stained skies
lead me down, the frozen keeper of my ruins
bores through me with the hell of my accusations
and leads me in handcuffs
in this monarchy of my canonized crimes!

In the Cities

I must keep coming back to the cities regardless
    and roam through my certifiably insane streets,
the crippled nights open wide with the madness of my limbs,
    letting whores down my trouser pockets to scatter
                                    tattered flowers
        over the left side of my heart.

Hidden in stinking guesthouses underneath a winter coat
                                          collar,
    singing my songs like psalms, I let the stars dance in
                                    endless mugs,
I go on foot in the frost through mountains of beef goulash
                                  with caraway,
    I pull the moon, my great master, from my soused shoe
and choose myself as the prince of every kingdoms to come.

Regardless I must keep coming back to the cities,
    to their subaltern districts, to rows of houses without
                            sleep writing down
under the bridges by the morbid bodies of canals
    a degraded life's insane books correcting
their desolation to be found in the factories, in the toilets of
                            neglected skies,
    the conditions of their regurgitated winter flogged
by the sharpness of the unceasing snow.

Daybreak (II)

Along with stray dogs I am more despicable to heaven
    than hell,
with temples torn apart unbarring the terrible sun
    in my brain

I am from the collarbone on down abandoned
    in the middle of the road of my demolished sleep.
In the giant skull of my religions I am buried
    in the scenes of my future desolation.

Snarled at by the storm wind, a bloody altar boy
    of bawling October streets,
dead already from weeping, sprawled in the whispers of my
                    ruined autumn.
    Suddenly, screamed at by the morning, I stand in a forest
                    of watchmen.

Dialogue

The maw of the people froths
    from the rainy autumn,
but you walk through the cold
    with the storm wind on your lips
and you are bound to nothing.

The maw of the people froths
    underneath the cloak of the sky,
not one look of gloom
    dare you leave alone,
saying nothing along with the winter cold
    you carry on your dialogue.

In subterranean cities
    you explain noon to these people,
with serenity you rule over them,
    who cobbled away the fatherland
on a tawdry Good Friday.

Fame

From the hills of my youth I look
down, I do not fear
the villages, the thunderstorms stamp in my brain,
the neighing of horses rushes in the vaults of water,
a shivering angel touches my brow and chooses me for his
                                                    brother,
in every river I am the lord of my floating sky,
the shabby days of apples and the family's wheat,

Truths are placed in my way, the traitor cripples
laugh over me,
in bestial forests I freeze, devouring my literal nonsense
in a pile of homesickness and agonizing prejudice,

with great army leaders I gather at the edges,
on the desolate squares of my wasteland,
with a toast master's throwing up and monotony,
with the wild card sting of my audacity,

conditions arise and set me right,
in great books my dictum rots down to the vermin of the
                                                    dead,
through every open grave I sharpen my prostrate conscience,
the wind and the unrest with mercy,

without having to leave myself, I choose myself,
an ancestor of the moles in abandoned meadows,
vaguely linked by marriage to the snouts of wild sows,
a snowstorm's baying on the fields sung white,

the houses of my great-grandparents barricade me,
                murmur me to nothing behind their doors,
black graves upon me of that haunting smell of death,

through the joints of the winter I learn my fame,
in the brooks and in the church bells,
the spring raped against the stonewalls rings
of its enormous resistance,

the dry tongue pounds on the wall of my cup,
my misshapen flesh eats away at the conventions I learnt,
when the spring does not befall in one blow with its moaning
                               and wailing,
which holds sway over the cities and rivers,

O were I no shame,
were I not betrayed by the traitors and not undersold by my
                               brothers,
infamous, a flock of hungry birds,
black and wild and alone above this country besung too much,

I appear before the cripples and the aristocrats
and deliberate on the loafers,
I am in this criminal cold to the death,

I tie the rope of my sins of omission to no human word,
make no step with a paralytic heaven,
alone without me and dead my breeders stand around me,

in the turning of my days I suffer nothing but the spring,
I suffocate in its lust for power, gone wild with the grass,
celebrated on these inaccessible peaks of fame.

Snowmelt

Hear only the water's fall!
From the slumber of a deadly humiliations
my clever heart is chilled, openly pounding in my chest.
The sea rises up and time and space are dashed to pieces!

           In the spring the grass tastes
of freshly washed dead, I hear spirited valleys,
blackbirds, falcons. The frozen hillsides are melting when the
                                turkey cock crows.
Where am I? Where? I hear:
April coming to me through the forests of jasmine.

Soon

My life is soon over,
    my love frost,
without farewell
    the clear night,

Limbs, the snow
    of a thousand years
killing me,
    I am enfeebled,

with grief
    the hills garland
me long
    before Christmas Eve.

Question

What am I day and night,
what day, what night, what am I
day and night, what night, what day?

What do I hear day and night,
what day and night, what do I hear
day and night, what night, what day?

What do I want day and night,
what day, what night, what do I want
day and night, what night, what day?

What are you day and night,
what day, what night, what are you
day and night, what night, what day?

I Prefer to Go Now

I prefer to go now
    to my grave
as though over and over
    back into the village,
no, no longer do I go
    where nothing waits for me ...

I prefer to go now
    to my grave
when I drink
    when I weep,
where I am nothing,
    was nothing.

I prefer to go now
    to my grave
for dying will
    not take me long,
just like my life was,
    already far too long.

No Tree (II)

For John Donne

No tree
will understand you,
no forest,
no river,

no frost,
not ice, not snow,
no winter, you,
no me,

No storm wind
on high, no grave,
not East, not West,
no weeping, woe,
no tree . . .

Ask the Dead at the Outskirts of the City

Ask the dead at the outskirts of the city,
ask the dead deep in the forest and ask the dead by the river,
ask the dead for their names and walk into the winter.

Ask snow and ice and ask the bridges,
ask the bushes and the swarms of birds,
ask father and mother, ask brother and sister,
ask the wind, ask the river, ask the silence.
Ask the dead at the outskirts of the city ...

Woodsmen

They all asked for the name of the winter,
knocked the mud from their boots at the front door and
                                    stormed the tables,
got drunk,
and each laid a girl,
such that the birds flew up into the air from their kissing,
                                                    warm.
In the barrels fermented their first thousand years, which
     made them as thoughtful as their stupid stomachs,
and they stared out into the countryside and were dead,
                              white, for death swallowed
them all down with its hammer,
crippled them and left nothing behind for their wails,
which soon, left all alone, choked them.
In the rising of the moon one discovered the tracks of the
                              Crow King among them
and rubbed his hands over the fire,
while the others were still in bed,
hanged on their dreams.

In the Bedroom

Just listen to the birds! Their flocks wailing,
they fly into rage from field to field;
the entire land is black and my heart is black too,
and blind from the grief my entrails bleed.

In the gloomy room the torment wears the stone
and fells whole forests of prior grief,
the boards cold, the bed sheet already rotten,
my brain goes through the wall dead.

Yes, I Am Dead

Yes, I am dead! The frost is to blame
that my weeping is stiff, my hand,
that my laughter
is stiff, my eyes,
that my laughter froze me to death,
yes, so fewer days to grieve,

yes, I am dead! The frost is to blame
that the yellow wheat in the grave is stiff,
the cold mother's word
that the wild grapevine froze along the wall,

yes, I am dead! The frost is to blame
that my weeping is stiff, my hand,
that my laughter is stiff, my eyes,
that my land froze me,
yes, so fewer days to grieve,
I am dead, the frost is to blame . . .

Human Fates

Human fates, do you not shiver
at their tables, in their beds, does your foot
not shiver in their house,
your head when their wits strike it dead,
your tongue, when they speak?

Human fates, you shiver
when sun and moon become twinned in their truth,

Frost, your mouth says to the summertime,
Frost, your cold hand writes, Frost,
where among human fates grief
enticed you into crying about yourself: Frost.

Above

A mindless, pointless falling of silence
                                above,
why do you cry the whole night and drink
                                yourself blue and blow yourself
up? Eh? Brains of a human vermin huckster? Eh . . . ?
                                So that your joints kill you off
with their screaming, all of which bores
                                above,
why do you cry the whole night and drink?
                                I never want to be me, you know
                                                me,
what the world hears, nothing knows,
                                everything alone is me,
the black night
                                without a star, me, without fame,
                                above.

Winter (II)

The harshness came without end
in the main thoroughfares and gathered itself on the squares
and drove man and dog together into a bloody ball,
such that the wind went astray in their heads
and the whole world was filled with howls against the harsh
god.

Alone on the street, I was the witness of a hereafter whom
no one summoned,
they had no concern for my exhaustion, much less for my
bad brain,
which warped and sick from madness and folly grew swollen
in the sky[.]

Not a single place in my verse did they know named me,
betraying to the dead my disgraced names, in all clarity
about me,
no cold, not the stanza of my forever humiliated fame!
My flesh crouched at their feet and I thought of their
children
and I knew of their dissolute world, the cold instilling them
with my abuse.

From one to the other I went without myself during my
coming days
and drowned my habitual ways in their houses, spitting from
their palaces,
I established a kingdom upon their kingdoms!

If I were ever from such a county, I would speak their
language
I would weep their weeping, as long as the earth shall
perish,
as long as my weeping shall perish for all eternity too . . .

Until I am blamed across the sky in their agony, I am the one
and only lord whom they experience
and in my imperfection this laudable exception for all time!

Insane with their backsliding I drive the holy winter across
the earth,
and as the frost flees from me, I fear nothing
but the shadows of my love in my drowned breast.

The Drinkers

A dark swarm of birds, they do not turn around,
death at their backs, in their shadows love
for no meal, nor for a bitter future,
who from their cups stick out their tongues and groan their
                                                    names.
in vaults, cold, ancient . . .
        The frost shone upon the limbs of their harshness
and plunged them into the snow and cold,
as the frostbitten howl, I hear the forests now
and the murderous intentions of great rivers, shrieking which
                                                    shakes me
to the marrow, on their lips
I dangle, buried in their solitude of death.

Alpha and Omega (I)

Me, my world, something I say: my days,
my lofty pain, my unlearnt measure,
my shadow-addicted mind, which toppled
what was upon me early on and let me run,
hurt . . .

    Not that the fame in my breast began to rot
and the stars came to me, sweeping prejudices . . .
A philosophy drove me dishevelled along the shore
and subjected my terrors in paternal discipline and love,
where soon falls silent what I knew no more . . .

    I wrote about myself and no one read to the end,
for everyone shivered and no one was like me . . .

    Still I go through cities numb and bleak
and layers of utter darkness rip open my wounds, which

                 have not healed
in all these long years,
and my pride is already strange and my sorrow plain,
the stupidity a psalm, which I hear in my half-sleep,
my soul's way pious, no more do I turn back,
unless I am summoned by my dead.

I Suffered from Shadows

I suffered from shadows and drunken husbands,
the wives teaching me to undress them
and ask no questions . . . soon I was numb and I did not
                                     becloud the days
after sunny and warm, ice-cold nights, menially sleeping
by a bucket of pig slop, often plucking the trees
and joking with the moon and the hungry owl
as I shivered with cold . . .
I suffered from shadows and dead, this I have known for a
                                     long time . . .
And no more oaths, no suffering mornings, house and home,
not that I did not drop dead . . . I walked around myself
and shovelled myself up and did not choose,
for what a man chooses crushes him without question,
and I sought my misery in dark holes
and found sleep and curled myself up into the stars.

I Go Down into the City

I go down into the city, where all are dead
and no one fights back like the moon in the stability of the
stars
not giving me a name, thus do I tell it to no one, not even
Death . . .
I am mad in their houses, Death, I say,
is before me and when I come back, it is enough that I give
a sign
to the dark forests, to the cold booze vaults,
I don't speak of my mother, weeping to my father
just like I was a companion for decades,

I do not want to die when the spring comes
and I scatter no misery in winter's furrows,
not a day am I alone and without myself
an endlessly proud grave on a black hill . . .

I go down into the city, at this time my memory is silent,
the storm wind's cold gathers in me
and from my eyes is the clear sense.

Time Has Reached the Bottom

Time has reached the bottom
    in this spring day, in the crowds,
in the market square,
    in the speeches of my centuries,
in the achievements of the earth,

time has reached the bottom in the people,
    in the conditions they are in,
such that their entrails shiver and their hearts
    stand still for a moment,
for a moment of the future.

Time has reached the bottom
    in the palaces
and in their deliberations,
    with a philosophical winter's harshness
it attacked their heads and feet
    and humiliated them,

time has reached the bottom
    in this spring day, in the crowd,
one stupid from gaping
    and sick from monotony, spitefully

which speaks against the destitute,
    which mirrors in countless rivers
the monotony of their souls.

Time has reached the bottom
    and cloaks itself
with the shame of its speech,
    protesting this infinite patience
and blotting out its experiences
    and not belonging to humanity.

Time has reached the bottom
    and made right,
in arid letters
    it performed its spectacle
on the slopes of apathy
    for every one of its underlings.

In the Spring

In the spring I lead the sacred streams
into temptation, furious errors
into the fields,
the astonishing toil of apple blossoms invoked.

In the spring I explain myself to my judges and am pulled
under where the grass in the morning scourged
my washed-to-death iniquity desecrating its green
for a rotten worm, for a jaw thought into the ground.

In the spring the plans of the creator are unclear to me
as at any other time of the year and the earth
opposes how I toss it in its condition
of my songs, which fall like the snow falls.

Down among the Fish of the Seas

Down among the fish of the seas
    you go on this spring day,
down into the oblivion of the palaces.
    No face ashamed as you speak
the language handed down to you
    deep below in the precincts of the dead.

In the rushing of the wind you raise
    the indictment against bad judges,
against morning and AMEN,
    such that every plaint erupts
with the tremendous cry of your torment.

Hear the Storm Wind

The word is but a sham, the swarm of birds
is alarm, the insects rustle, the stalls scrape
at what death and murder and eternal murder owe,
the winter's harsh snow pays, where I amass the wailing,
roosters crow horribly mutilated,
disreputably, a murder, a crippled hand, describes
and delivers you deaf and listless, who see, die . . .
hear the storm wind,
      hear what it says,
            where its word is only deceit . . .

Stand Up and Speak

Stand up and speak of the sexes,
of darkness and the holy cold of death,
in great classrooms teach them to die
in the spring, in the stammering of the storm.

Stand up and speak the language of their dead,
from the green hills proclaim yourself below,
You, solitude, a vile copulation!

Every Day

Every day you must go through the vermin of the dead,
left alone in the neglect you shiver on a chain of hills,
if only my winter coat did not feel so tight
and on my cap are the long dead names as well,
my boots pinch me, the sweaty rags of a corpse!

Every day I must go through the vermin of the dead,
their odious insinuations drive me below into the
royal majesty of the butchering,
such that I am a man made of their flesh and blood,
I cannot forgive a dog, let alone them!

Every day I must go through the vermin of the dead,
with this self-righteous precision driving my ruined life,
beating my ridiculed back,
the drunken mouth bloody before the flowers!

In July

In July I am stiff and dead and irreconcilable,
a mad-dog wind tore my miserable earth apart,
I am sworn to this time of every reeking condition!

In July I descend into the graves and remove
the human heads, their stupid moonstruck wailing,
below I am eaten away by the hunger and the love
forever wedged between the flesh of their defeats!

The War

The war destroyed me, I still hear the war
in the forests and the rivers,
the tassels of wheat are shaken by my prayers,

you pass your freezing days in the spat-upon city
and you see the flames lick at the udders of the spring!

A battered time, which passes through me and erases my
                                                    questions,
the churches standing left alone by the sun, black,
monuments of this annihilated mind!

This continual time rose in the cups of the ears
and ripped out the entrails,
the bloody streams' madness leading us to glory.

Defiance

The winter says, I am dead,
in the fevers of the earth I lie, mutilated,
crazy,
the winter says, I am dead,

a sack stabbed to pieces, the dirty worm
of their skullcaps, there, where the frost advances
against its enemies with its club . . .
the winter says, I am dead . . .

    . . . the maw of the war and stupidity engorged,
I bleat my sheepish curse
on the winter.

My Land

My land is utterly dark and where the cows yawn
there is utter darkness in my land too,
the orations go from one pig to another,
when the rain showers down,
everyone crawls deep into their beds.

My land is utterly dark and no man goes
in the night without a knife in his pocket,
often frightened by a defiant pheasant,
a warlike character,
throwing his life into the biting stream.

With furtive looks they deny
any familiarity with God's blessing,
their wheat is music, their slaughtered cattle tough
from being beaten, their voices coarse, their hearts
hard, alone, with no echo.

My land is utterly dark and where the cows yawn
there is utter darkness in my land too,
their udders hang on the sky, yet
devilish hands pull on them and draw
forth a deadly milk into the pails.

When the Nights Were Not (*II*)

When the nights were not, I would be dead,
given how they howled inside me, the dogs
make my brain and bones ring full of misery
from my stupid year, such that my hands tremble
and the grass must burn, the towers lance
pus from the belly of the sky, the rivers burst.

When the nights were not, I would be dead,
torn apart by the wheel along with the dead
in the leprosy of their agony, the fields hounding, hissing
in the winter leaves, thoughts of nature splattering black
on my face, the land, the city,
the way of things groaning in milky bosom sweat.

When the nights were not, I would be dead,
joints of slaughtered cattle, whispers
of birds gone astray, a growling of the elements,
restless worms and a nation of cats, a lock-jawed,
subterranean prominence of decay!

London

City of cities! Remain behind me, with the years
    the sea taught me the beginnings of winter, cost me
                      the death
of my friend nature, monuments of gigantic, primal
                      experience,
    limitless in catacombs I knew nothing of wheat,
    nothing of the blackish hillsides, the insanity's
                      unapproachable future
shuddered below me, railways dissect the desert island,
    torn by streams of people, I gaped into the night in
                      uncounted beds,
without joy, perished in the steady plod of the English,
    floated through a sullen sky, my anger robbed of its
                      severity,
I pitied myself on the green coastlines.

Torrents of agony, a cocky volubility, I froze to death
    amid their laughter, destroyed by their computations,
                      staggering sleepless
through the centuries, searched fields of grass in a winter
                      coat made of hate
    for their cold, statues bleated at me, this self-
                      opinionated void
yawned down from the paintings of the masters, my

stupid awe assuming a state of mourning,
patronized by the clear nights, I dined with myself on
a deserted log,
I wrote letters to this raped valley while every incurable
disease attacked me.

In underground vaults I staggered by the memorials to the
dead,
I explored bomb-proof tunnels, survived with my brains
smashed,
soaked in the frost of grief carpentered with innocent
pieces of advice,
amid all of their shaking voices I mixed my voice,
amid all their prayers I mixed my prayers, travelling along
the bottom of the sea,
with my uncomprehending shadow in tow, I chained myself
to their public-house laughter,
the cursing lowlands shuddered under my legs, the
furious trains sliced through my melancholy's rope,
a grey sky's monotony took its revenge on my otherwise
resourceful math.

Incompetent gobbets of Jesus and holy Jerusalem buried
my wretched foothold,
swept up by beer I discovered the centre of the cities,
with eyes on fire I felt their udders, I reaped the morass of
stars,
inaccessible meadows, tied up the wheat, plunged my
hands in the river water,
beat myself down to a pile of crushed meat,

such that dying would be glorious, decrepitude a royal
                                        simplification,
      I learnt that the squandering-addicted moon hung in
                            my mouth and spoke to me,
    'I am incompetent, he always said, incompetent, always
                                        incompetent!'
I was abandoned from the very first hour, with biting coat
                                        pockets
I stood before my judges and did not understand their
                                        language.

In this famous air I choked, whispers assaulted me, the
                                        vomiting
of tens of thousands of relationships, in the garden of
                      Westminster I touched the sky
and was bayed back! In the deadly silence of thousands
                of years I placed my condemned head,
and ran sleeping through entire races of people, an
                    inconspicuous army of oppressors,
broken on the wheel of this storm of immortality, I
                    received my British baptism,
    the floodgates of experience opened, rushing rain swept
                      over the precincts of my thoughts;
for I am now closer than ever to the forests, gigantic
                                catafalques of bread,
    the rustling of the meadows, unearthly streams,
waking up in the dampness of a defeated morning!

Me, My World (II)

Me, my world, something I say: my days,
my lofty A and O, my unlearnt measure,
my shadow–addicted mind, which toppled
what was on me early on and let me go,
hurt . . .
Not that the fame in my breast began to rot
and the stars came to me, sweeping prejudices . . .
An idea drove me dishevelled along the shore
and I subjected my terrors in paternal discipline and love,
where soon will fall silent that which I knew no more . . .
I wrote about myself and no one read to the end,
for everyone shivered and no one was like me . . .
Still I go through cities numb and bleak
and layers of utter darkness rip open my wounds, which
                                        have not healed
in all these long years,
my pride is already strange, my sorrow plain,
the stupidity a psalm, which I hear in my half-sleep,
pious, my soul's price, no more do I turn back now,
unless I am summoned by my dead.

My God

My God,
        You walk into these terrible conditions,
in this almighty sleep, in streets full of people,
mightily whipped by their misery, You Yourself know
of their sleazy lies of their treacherous hymns,
of their outright pleading and begging, which swells with
                             the rivers,
such that time stands still in the squares, in the churches
                             and palaces!

My God,
        the damaged tracts of land quake under Your
                             judgement,
my bones are ground and turned to dust, my bed is in
                             disarray
from Your madness, from Your ruin every Sunday!
In the stormy bushes my joints cool, for I was astonished
over You and knelt in the encounter and did not hesitate,
to redeem myself, my terrifyingly wounded soul!

Do Not Lift My Sleep

Do not lift my sleep,
    where the veil, soiled by the grave, beats wild roses,
be satisfied that I screamed in anger last night:
    long ago I let myself go, long ago
and I cared nothing for myself, long ago dead, I let myself
                        run, a mangy dog . . .

Do not lift my sleep,
    it is over, what I was, I do not want, such that a friend
                        mourns for me,
what does anyone know? what pulls them down then?

I am not related to snow and ice, there is nothing but hate
                        about it,
    something I tell the winter: you, grief . . .

Do not lift my sleep,
    the whole valley is stupid, and its meadows are white,
the forest rustles apart, the streams are frostbitten . . .
    no likeness of cow and ox . . . no blacker lot
than standing on the bridge and then: freezing to death!

In the First Snow

A useless world in your brain, you hesitate
    to see the black forest, the dark farms,
the whole valley, stirred into a frenzy
    and goaded fields, morally dead,
a common hand gesture of grand heavenly princes,
    a hall cruelly scrubbed apart, a decrepit church steeple's
                                   plaints,
I want nothing any more, I mean nothing to you,
    the dreams are dismembered, a storm wind's drive
delved into my parents for me, children, stinking beds.
    The stench of the time amassed from the house pets,
the hate blew me with countless ailments
    down by the river. Frightened in the garbage
of abandoned souls I am disgusted by the nausea
    of one's own grief in the falling flakes.

Eminent Innkeepers

Eminent innkeepers await you
    when you go down to the dead in August,
speck sausages crack, awash in beer . . .
    which your forefathers did not call despair . . .
        Thus must many an old man
feel shame to be at your side,
    when you cut yourself a generous slice
of fat from heaven for a poor mercantile soul
    and drink to your father,
whom you discover at his green table
    in the rear of those vaults
much greater than anything ever on earth!

Autumn

With my laments
    the streams and the rivers fill,
I go down into sleep
    with the birds
and sick from weeping . . .

an empty house
    and a freezing heart,
I am in every room
    dying over my grave,
the crown prince
    of my drunken songs.

October Storm

Is this sea not chained
to my mind? Are not the blossoms
of dark forests showering
fear and anger driven through me by an October storm?
                    How long is time and how long am I in it?
What am I now, since yesterday
dead, at the end? I never counted the cities, never the space
and did not grow old in them, which I always hated ...
                    For this storm frightened me, I saw my life
as hopeless and I was dead, never before so dead,
as though I had never lived, never seen a day, never a night
forsaken, never loved,
never yet afraid of my country!

Is this sea not chained
to my mind? Are not the blossoms
of dark forests showering
fear and anger driven through me by an October storm?

Do You Hear the Madness of My Cold (*II*)

Do you hear the madness of my cold? Are you
    not shivering? The stiffened foot, which you must
watch in battle, like its older brother
    torn apart in the evening sky boding dark marches
and melting away like sleep?

      Do you hear the madness? A jog-trot of
                    commanding generals
through my brainsick blood, straining battle ranks
screaming? With impotence you fight a war and with
             heads bleak cemetery walls . . .

      In the driving snow your mouth and thighs
gape from weeping,
    no king takes revenge on your hands,
the error of your grief, the broken curses
    embroiling you in night and howls, cup and horrors,
such that your flesh falls exhausted from your soul
    startled in the moon, the grim earth

betrays this human madness, shattered by agony!

I Am Freezing

I am freezing,
the winter on the slope pulls
my joints together, all the misery
    of my battered years.

I am freezing,
senile tree, worn-out lie
of my pain!, the valleys' scream
    from the tatters of a shroud . . .

I am freezing,
I must go down and in the land
tear open an eternal earth with bare bones,
to perform its humble work,
    to leave my love behind.

Conversation with the Paris Moon

I

An imbecile, a priest,
a mirror image of my sleep!

Heaven and hell, hell
and heaven am I, a man in neglect!

The blood's grief from madness
black, the streets stinking

stupidly of speck, a creature, awash
in beer, the night devious!

An indisposed woman, an apathetic,
an amputated leg, a bib-fly ruiner,

the kings skip out on me, medals, chorales
of endless madness! I am heard

by a swarm of birds on the river, the devilish pimps
giving me a thrashing!

II

On my bed her neglected heart
casts me into darkness! Her temples

are drunken from purity, her face
is unbearable as the winter!

I rise up early, so that her torment
hears me, her claws crown me!

What is this utter, blasphemous darkness,
what is killing me? Is that my coat? Are those

my boots? To her earrings I want
my ruin chained forever!

III

My flesh has grown accustomed to sleepless nights,
not my soul,

not my land, a raving mad delirium's
laws of gravity humiliated me!

I am sick from perfectly healthy meadows,
put-up job fields, the weals of the Milky Way!

Wordlessly I listen, unable to defend
myself and my rundown community,

bloody from the sharpened grass

I am incurably ill
on the streets of the miserable, of the raving mad!
    My eyes are cities,
my ears storms! A licentious defence

is my body! And you give my brain
no peace, there, where I am my only monument,

a childhood of future paradises,
a murderous superstition's confusion!

Where?

O pain, when the world drowned in fog
clings to your forsaken brain, the dog
howls at the door, the beds creak with people
who are dead, every day dead, dead, dead,

the way the snow falls on me, the way hair gives me a
            beating,
 the shadow makes signs on the wall, which frightens me
            whenever
I go into my room, whenever,

O pain, where I find myself, and I am not dead, where
I find my days now, where I my time,
where I an answer once, where I always asked?

Alpha and Omega (III)

Me, my world, something I say: my days,
my lofty A and O, my unlearnt measure,
my shadow-addicted mind, which toppled
what was on me early on and let me run,
hurt . . .

     Not that the fame in my breast began to rot
and the stars came to me, sweeping prejudices . . .
A philosophy drove me dishevelled along the shore
and subjected my terrors in paternal discipline and love,
where soon falls silent what no one on earth knows any
                     more . . .
     I wrote about myself and no one read to the end,
for everyone shivered and no one was like me . . .

     Still I go through cities numb and bleak
and layers of utter darkness rip open my wounds, which
                    have not healed
in all these long years.
My pride is already strange, my sorrow plain,
the stupidity a psalm, which I hear in my half-sleep . . .
sick, my soul's price, no more do I turn back now,
not unless I am summoned by my dead.

Notes

Dates in parentheses appended to individual poems indicate the year of first publication.

Roman numerals in parentheses indicate the version of the poem.

Page 3 • 'My World Play'

Title, *My World Play* (*Mein Weltenstück*), the meaning here suggests both a work of art that is a 'vast' world unto itself, a work, that is, which the artist sees as speaking to the world and so worthy of the world canon (in the way Wagner's Ring Cycle is) and, too, a work in miniature, which can be seen in whole.

Page 7 • 'Fisherman on the Chiemsee'

Title, *Chiemsee*, a large lake in the Rosenheim district of Bavaria.

Page 8 • 'All Souls'

Dedication, *Agatha Wibe* (1871–1955), a Norwegian woman who corresponded with Bernhard's maternal grandfather, the writer Johannes Freumbichler.

485

Page 18 • 'In the Courtyard of St Peter's'

Title, *St Peter's*, a Benedictine monastery in Salzburg.

Page 19 • 'Cemetery in Seekirchen (I)'

Title, *Seekirchen*, i.e. Seekirchen am Wallersee, a town near Salzburg.

Stanza 2, omitted in the second version.

Page 21 • 'St Sebastian in Linzergasse'

Title, *St Sebastian*, a church and cemetery in Salzburg.

Line 12, Paracelsus (1493–1541), the Renaissance physician, is buried under the porch of St Sebastian.

Page 22 • 'Cloister Walk in Nonnberg Abbey'

Title, *Nonnberg Abbey* (*Kloster Nonnberg*), a Benedictine monastery in Salzburg founded in the year 714.

Page 29 • 'Cloister (II)'

Second version of 'Cloister Walk in Nonnberg Abbey'.

Page 32 • 'You Unknown Fathers of My Fame'

Excised from the manuscript of *On Earth and in Hell*.

Line 3, *Plaike mountain sky* (*Plaikenhimmel*), i.e. Grosse Plaike, near Henndorf am Wallersee.

Page 33 • 'Song for Young Males'

Line 27, *go hide* (*verstecken*), the German means to hide, but implicit is the sense of stuffing or thrusting something out of sight, i.e. idiom for anal intercourse.

Page 35 • On Earth and in Hell

Auf der Erde und in der Hölle (Salzburg: Otto Müller, 1957).

486

Charles Péguy (1873–1914), French poet. The epigram is taken from *Das Mysterium der Hoffnung* (1952), p. 127, the German translation of Péguy's *Le Porche du Mystère de la Deuxième Vertu* (1912) [The Portal of the Mystery of the Second Virtue, i.e. hope].

Page 41 • 'My Great-Grandfather Was a Lard Merchant'

Lines 4 and 5, *Henndorf and Thalgau,/Seekirchen and Köstendorf*, rural villages to the east of the city of Salzburg in the Salzburg-Umgebung or Flachgau district.

Line 20, *speck*, Austrian smoke-cured ham or lard flavoured with juniper berries and spices and cut into thin slices, cf. prosciutto.

Page 46 • 'Rot'

Line 4, *fame* (*Ruhm*), a keyword in Bernhard's poetry that should not be confused with 'fame' as it is understood in the way a politician or film actor is 'famous'. Here fame is simply a matter of presence. It is closer to Heidegger's sense vis-à-vis Hölderlein, who saw the fame and glory of gods and poets in terms of being allowed to appear (*Erscheinenlassen*), i.e. to be made real.

Page 56 • 'Crows'

Line 3, *corn schnapps* (*Körner*), i.e. rye whiskey or *Kornbranntwein*.

Page 64 • 'An Evening'

Line 12, *snow covered to their necks* (*Schnee im Genick*), lit. *snow in the neck*, an Austrian expression that can only be rendered paraphrastically, ironic since the idiom is associated with fun activities such as sledding or skiing.

Page 68 • 'In My Capital'

Line 3, *Hofburg*, the Hofburg Palace in Vienna, once the seat of government of the Hapsburg emperors.

Line 6, *Metternich*, Prince Klemens Wenzel von Metternich (1773–1859).

Page 71 • 'Paris'

Epigraph, *Your tears . . . (Dein Weinen . . .')*. from 'La Saison des amours' (Season of Love) by the French poet Paul Éluard (1895–1952)

Line I:16, *à la fin tu es las de ce monde ancient (in the end you are weary of this ancient world)*, from the poem 'Zone' by Guillaume Apollinaire.

Line I:17, *poets of the pavilions (Dichter der Pavillons)*, i.e. hospital patients, not the French poets named in the poem

Line IV:18, *blowing police whistles (in Trillerpfeifen blasen)*, slang for fellatio.

Line V:5, '*Valéry, . . . Coty,* the poet Paul Valéry (1871–1945) . . . René Coty, the president of France (1954–1959).

Line V:6, '*Notre nature est dans le mouvement . . .*'?, from Pascal's *Pensées*, NO. 129, which properly reads 'Our nature consists in movement; absolute rest is death' (*e repos entier est la mort*).

Line VI:16, *Avenue de Ternes*, an avenue in the 17th arrondissement of Paris.

Page 78 • 'Venice'

Line 5, *Maria della Salute*, the basilica of St Mary of Health; *Ca' d'Oro*, literally, the 'golden house,' a palace on the Grand Canal.

Line 6, *Colleoni*, the equestrian statue of Bartolemeo Colleoni (1400–75), captain-general of the Republic of Venice, by artist Andrea del Verrocchio (1435–88); *Palazzo Ducale*, the palace of the Doge.

Line 9, *Giorgione*, the painter Giorgio Barbarelli da Castelfranco (*c*.1477–1510).

Line 12, 'La Tempesta,' *c*.1508, considered the first landscape in Western art.

Page 79 • 'Chioggia'

Title, *Chioggia*, a commune of the province of Venice.

Page 93 • 'The Night'

Line 3, *day's work* (*Tagwerk*), an agrarian measure for an acre of land, also how much work can be done to it in a day (ploughing, mowing, etc.).

Page 113 • 'Before Bryant's Fame'

Title, *Bryant*, William Cullen Bryant (1794–1878), American poet, and author of a well-known meditation on death, *Thanatopsis* (1817), and editor of a three-volume *Complete Works of Shakespeare* (1886). Johannes Freumbichler is the likely conduit for both Bryant and Shakespeare in Bernhard's readings of English literature and Bernhard certainly revered the latter given the ironic pronouncements of two alter-egos–narrators–monologists in his later fiction. For example, Reger in *Old Masters*: *A Comedy* (1985), states: 'Shakespeare crumbles totally if we concern ourselves with him and study him for any length.' In *The Loser* (1983), a similar low opinion is expressed: 'Even Shakespeare shrivels down to something ridiculous for us in a clearheaded moment, he said, I thought.'

Page 115 • 'Black Hills'

Line 21, '*The sea . . . ,*' (*Das Meer ist groß, auch sind die Wüsten unerschöpflich, / und leidet sich's nicht besser fern von diesen Orten . . . ?*), the source of these lines is unknown.

Page 117 • 'Living and Dead'

Line 13, *the singular one* (*dem Einzelnen*), likely ironic, an allusion to individuality in the dialectic of Kierkegaard, Hegel, Nietzsche, Buber, et al.

Line 18, *forty-sixth summer,* an allusion to the death of the poet's mother Herta Fabjan (1904–1950).

Line 36, *well-pole* (*Brunnenschwanz*), a rare compound that can also mean the lever of a hand pump and a draw-well's pole.

Page 121 • 'Beyond the Wheat'

Line 13, *battered skulls* (*zerschundenen Schädel*), possibly a euphemism for philosophers.

Line 25, *houses of joy* (*Freudenhäusern*), brothels.

Page 130 • 'The Wind Blowing Spoke to These Fields'

Line 6, *dead days* (*Totentage*), days of inactivity.

Page 132 • 'Death and Thyme'

Title, *Thyme* (*Thymian*), the herb is traditionally associated with funerary rites, either burnt or placed on coffins to ensure safe passage into the next life.

Line 14, *church fair trumpets* (*Kirchtagstrompeten*), despite the religious connotation, such musical instruments announced a day more devoted to secular entertainments.

Lines 15–16, *trombones of smoked ham . . . sausages crack* (*Selchfleischposaunen . . . Würste krachen*), possibly a trope for flatulence.

Page 142 • 'I Must Go Back into the Village'

Line 5, *Hit that cider and funeral ham* (*Hau dich hin zu Most und Totenschinken*), an expression alluding to the apple must and ham served at the wake meal (*Trauermahle, Leichenessen*).

Page 149 • 'Altentann'

Title, *Altentann*, a hamlet near Henndorf am Wallersee.

Page 153 • 'My Father'

Line 1, *dryness of the soil* (*Dürre der Erde*), this dated phrase, repeated through the poem, can be found in nineteenth-century commentaries on the Book of Job as well as sermons and the like that compare the spiritual and human condition to harsh climates.

Page 157 • 'From Now On I Will Go into the Forest'

Line 4, *Corpus Christi* (*Fronleichnamstag*), a feast day and procession that occurs in the late spring in honour of the Holy Eucharist.

Line 7, *without fire . . . salt* (*ohne Feuer . . . Salz*), cf. Mark 9:49, 'For everyone will be salted with fire and every sacrifice will be salted with salt.'

Page 159 • *In Hora Mortis*

In Hora Mortis (Salzburg: Otto Müller, 1958). This title is taken from the closing line of the Latin version of the Hail Mary, 'nunc et in hora mortis nostrae' ('now and at the hour of our death').

Page 183 • *Under the Iron of the Moon*

Unter dem Eisen des Mondes (Cologne: Kipenheuer & Witsch, 1958). The title is suggested by Scene 21 in Georg Büchner's play *Woyzeck*, in which Marie observes the redness of the moonrise before her murder.

Page 198 • 'The rain of these days'

Line 11, *chin . . . dream*, an allusion to the 'chin count' of syllables, i.e. writing verse.

Page 220 • 'Come under the tree, there the dead'

Line 14, *singing sticks* (*singenden Stöcken*), i.e. walking or mountain-climbing sticks and their rhythmic sound.

Page 231 • 'The sea is a shadow of my DEATH'

Line 11, *Mogador*, historic name of the Moroccan city and beach resort of Essaouira on the Atlantic coast.

Page 248 • 'Speak grass'

Line 2, *peg to peg* (*Pflock zu Pflock*), a trope, perhaps as in a stringed instrument; *roots* (*Wurzeln*), a variant of this poem, 'In the Grass (Im Gras)' substitutes *moss* (*Moos*).

Line 6, *of the dead* (*der Toten*), the variant substitutes of *the brood* (*der Brut*).

Page 251 • The Insane   The Inmates

Die Irren   Die Häftlinge (Klagenfurt: privately printed, 1962).

Page 254 • 'The Insane' [first canto]

Line 3, *nun tails white* (*Nonnenschwänze weiß*), perhaps the distinctive habit of the Daughters of Charity of the asylum at Schwarzach-Schermberg, especially the headpiece, a large, starched swallowtail-like cornette.

Page 263 • 'The Inmates' [third canto]

Lines 1 and 2, *You have no spade . . . knaves of bells*, there are allusions in these two verses to cards in the (standard)

French and German decks, with the result that any card will do in an attempt to beat the hand here—the bells of knaves—in a metaphorical game of skat. In the first line of the stanza, three cards are named: a spade (*Pik*), diamond (*Karo*) and green ace (*Gras*). The latter is rendered from the contraction *Gras* (grass) for *Grün Ass* (green ace). The 'knaves of bells' is a compromise as rendered, for in the German deck there are two kinds of jacks or knaves: an upper (*Ober*), which equals the queen in a French deck, and the lower (*Unter*), which serves as a jack. These are trickster cards because they can trump the other face cards as well as an ace.

Line 14, *turtledove madness* (*Turteltaubenwahnsinn*), as one critic noted, 'a priceless metaphor for the evil eye of this limbo's observer.'

Page 266 • 'The Insane' [fourth canto]

Schermberg, an insane asylum (*Irrenanstalt*) in Schwarzach-Schermberg, Upper Austria operated by the Daughters of Charity.

Page 267 • 'The Inmates' [fourth canto]

Garsten, a town Upper Austria, site of a former Benedictine monastery that serves as penitentiary.

Page 269 • Ave Virgil

Ave Vergil (Frankfurt am Main: Suhrkamp, 1981).

Page 271 • 'Wedding Party'

Line 2, counter-names (*Widernamen*), cf. aliases.

Line 32, *Raftery*, the Irish Gaelic bard Anthony Raftery (1779–1835).

Line 35, '. . . *and death will never come / near us, forever not in the sweet wood . . .*', from Raftery's poem 'The Heart of the Forest.'

Line 93, *Zell*, a town on Lake Zell in the state of Salzburg.

Page 277 • 'Winter Morning'

Line 40, '*alphabet of Virgil . . . my farmers*,' Virgil is honoured here as father of the Bernhard's language and themes of rural life and social commentary.

Page 287 • 'Grief'

Line 102, *Catullus* (85–54 BCE), Roman poet born in Verona.

Page 297 • 'Your Death Is Not My Death'

Line 4, *Hymn to Mercury, hymn to Aldebaran*, Orphic hymns; the 'Hymn to Mercury' celebrates the god's role as a psychopomp, the guide of souls to Hades; the 'Hymn to Aldebaran' is associated with the conjunction of the star and the Sun thousands of years ago with the Magnus Annus—the Great Year—which saw the Golden Age end and the beginning of that periodical cycle of steady deterioration in which the world will end in a universal catastrophe.

Page 307 • 'Who in This City'

Line 24, *Karakorum/Mönchsberg*, Mönchsberg is a hill and fortress that overlooks Salzburg, the city in this poem. Bernhard has ironically juxtaposed it to the ruined Mongol capital of Karakorum in Mongolia.

Line 33, *Residenz*, a baroque palace and seat of the regional government in Salzburg.

Page 327 • 'Psalm'

The stanzaic form of the recited under the variant title 'Whisper' (*Geflüster*) on the Austrian radio network ORF in April 1960.

Page 329 • 'Bible Scenes'

Dedication, Georges Roualt (1871–1958), French expressionist painter who painted numerous devotional images.

Page 343 • 'Slaughtering Day Night'

Line 3, *stockman's apron* (Hütertuch), cf. to butcher's apron.

Page 345 • 'At the Thurn Pass'

Title, *Thurn Pass*, mountain pass in Austria in the Kitzbühel Alps which connects the provinces of Tyrol and Salzburg.

Page 350 • 'I Feel the Moon's Too Good'

Epigraph, from *Hamlet*, Act 5, Scene 1.

Page 351 • 'No One Knows You'

Epigraph, *My feast of joy* (*Vom Freudenmahl*) . . .

Line 2 from 'Tichborne's Elegy' by the English Catholic conspirator and poet Chidiock Tichborne (1562?–1586), written on the night before his execution.

Page 353 • 'Skull Cider'

Line 44, *skull cider* (Schädelmost), an ironic neologism that imparts the process (crushed fruit) as well as mental intoxication.

Page 357 • 'To W. H. (I)'

See note for p. 373, 'To H. W. (II)'.

Page 358 • 'Horse Traders, Farmers, Grenadiers (I)'

First version of 'Description of a Family'.

Page 360 • 'Guard Me'

Line 1, *east and west* (*Osten und Westen*), the binary here suggests the Austrian state as much as personhood, that and the tension of the Cold War divide.

Line 2, *regulators* (*Regulierer*), a title, given the context, for various kinds of traffic controllers (road, rail, river, air), cf. the once ubiquitous military traffic police of East Germany.

Page 362 • 'In the Valley'

Line 9, *N.W.*, possibly the abbreviation of Neumarkt am Wallersee, a rural town in the Flachgau region northwest of Salzburg. In Bernhard's early life, his missing father, Alois Zuckerstätter, had worked there. It was his last known address.

Page 364 • 'A Stanza for Padraic Colum'

Title, *Padraic Colum* Padraic Colum (1881–1972), Irish poet and playwright.

Subtitle, *Across the Door*, a poem from Colum's first book *Wild Earth* (1916) that describes the pleasure of a young girl's first encounter with the power of sex.

Line 8, *Zell* [am See], a town on Lake Zell in the Austrian state of Salzburg; *Caliban*, Prospero's antagonist in Shakespeare's *The Tempest*.

Page 365 • 'Birthday Ode'

Line 9, *cover* (*Decken*), in this context, to stud.

Line 11, year of Bernhard's birth.

Line 14, *hammers* (*Totschläger*), cf. a pig or cow hammer, a bludgeon to humanely kill livestock before slaughter, *zinc hooks* (*Zinkhaken*), meat hooks.

Page 372 • 'In silva salus'

Title, *In silva salus*, a Latin motto (in the forest lies safety or salvation) that resonates in Germany–Austria for it recommends the benefits of the forest retreat that is here a negative experience.

Epigraph, *King: Though yet of Hamlet . . .*, the first two lines of King Claudius' speech that beings Act I, Scene 2 of *Hamlet*.

Page 373 • 'To H.W. (II)'

Based on a dedication to the poem 'Selchdritt' ('Smoked Threesome', as in meat) in the unpublished manuscript of *Frost*, H.W. are the initials for a 'dead butcher brother, war veteran, and friend'.

Page 374 • 'No Tree (I)'

Epigraph, *A reason for John Donne* (*Ein Ursache für John Donne*), on interpreting this seemingly impenetrable lyric, one must consider that here that the negation–annihilation of *Heimat*, *Natur*, and *Ich* (ego) provide a rationale, indeed, the void, the mental space for Donne (i.e. love and metaphysical poems) as well as solace.

Page 375 • 'Two Beer Bottles and an Ice Stock'

Title, *Ice Stock* (*Eisstock*), an ice curling stone with a long, upright handle.

Line 11, *foot-word wretch, chin-count cheater* (*Fußwörterschuft, Kinnverzähler*), i.e. one who shortchanges or fakes the metrical feet and syllable counts of his verses.

Line 19, *starset* (*Sternuntergegang*), the opposite of starrise.

Page 376 • 'Kitzlochklamm'

Title, *Kitzlochklamm*, a gorge of steep canyons and waterfalls formed by the Rauris River in the state of Salzburg.

Dedication, *Rafael Alberti* (1902–1999), Spanish poet.

Page 399 • 'Paranoia?'

Bernhard wrote his last poem for a New Year's Day feature in *Die Zeit*, 1982.

Line 27, *Café Draxelmayer, Café Traxlmayr*, a famous coffee house in Linz, Austria.

Line 30, *Rapid* and *LASK*, Vienna and Linz's rival football teams respectively.

Line 54, *Golden Roof* (*Goldenen Dachl*), a sixteenth-century landmark building in the centre of Innsbruck, Austria, with a large, open oriel shingled with copper tiles.

Page 405 • '1931'

Title, *1931*, Thomas Bernhard's birth year.

Line 4, *district inspector* (Rayonsinspecktor), a policeman in Austria's regional gendarmie.

Page 406 • 'On the Kapuziernberg'

Title, *Kapuziernberg*, a hill on the eastern bank of Salzach River in Salzburg which is named for Capuchin monastery there.

Line 11, *security police* (*Sicherheitswachebeamte*), i.e. the former Austrian federal police corps, whose officers wore uniforms of a military pattern to distinguish them from municipal police.

Line 12, *Elective Affinities, The Elective Affinities* (*Die Wahlverwandtschaften*, 1809), the third novel by Johann Wolfgang von Goethe, based on the metaphor of human passions being governed by the laws of chemical affinity and whether the laws of chemistry undermine or uphold human social relations such as marriage and friendship.

Line 13, '*There was a king in Thule*', the first line from Goethe's 1774 poem 'Der König in Thule' (The King in Thule) which he later incorporated into his *Faust*.

Page 411 • 'Decay (I)'

Variant of 'When the Nights Were Not (II)', p. 466.

Page 416 • 'After the Verdict'

The title is inferred, the original being 'First Day on the Job'.

Line 11, *Omen Days* (*Lostage*), literally, 'days of fate', the holiday period of the twelve days of Christmas between 25 December and 6 January and, in German and Austrian folklore, those days following the winter solstice on which future events, such as the weather, can be predicted.

Line 12, *forced labour* (*Frondienst*), cf. *corvee*, obligatory or compulsory work for the state.

Page 420 • 'I Feel the Moon's Too Good (II)'

Epigraph, from *Hamlet*, Act 5, Scene 1.

Page 426 • 'North and South'

Epigraph, from 'Le voyage' in *Fleur du mal*:

We have seen stars
And waves; we have seen too sandy wastes;
And despite many a shock and unforeseen
Disaster, we were often bored, as we are here.

Line II.2, Empedocles (*c.*490–*c.*430 BCE) of Agrigentum (Agrigento, Sicily), the Greek pre-Socratic philosopher.

Page 433 • 'Dialogue'

Lines 15–16, *cobbled away . . . Good Friday* (*verschustert . . . Karfreitag*), *verschustern* is idiom similar in meaning to *potter* or *putter away*. Good Friday, i.e. as a bank holiday, leisure time.

Page 441 • 'No Tree (II)'

Epigraph, *A reason for John Donne* (*Ein Ursache für John Donne*), on interpreting this seemingly impenetrable lyric, one must consider that the negation–annihilation of *Heimat*, *Natur* and *Ich* (ego) provides a rationale, indeed, the void, the mental space for Donne (i.e. love and metaphysical poems) as well as solace.

Page 451 • 'Alpha and Omega (I)'

First version.

Page 465 • 'When the Nights Were Not (II)'

Variant of 'Decay' (Fäulnis), p. 411.

Page 466 • 'London'

Line 32, *royal simplification* (*königliche Vereinfachung*), irony, as in a maths problem or equation.

Page 469 • 'Me, My World (II)'

Second version of 'Alpha and Omega (I)', see p. 451.

Page 472 • 'In the First Snow'

Line 5 *heavenly princes* (*Himmelsfürsten*), an honorific extended to archangels, church fathers, saints and so on.

Page 476 • 'Do You Hear the Madness of My Cold (II)'

Second version of 'Battle (I)', p. 428.

Page 482 • 'Alpha and Omega (III)'

Third version of 'Alpha and Omega (I)', see p. 451.

With gratitude and affection,
this book is for Heinz Wohlers.